AF701560

Financial Crisis

Causes and Solutions

F. T. Haner

PRAEGER

New York
Westport, Connecticut
London

Dedicated to
Dee Harris Haner,
the person who had all the wonderful
critical comments and constructive suggestions

Library of Congress Cataloging in Publication Data

Haner, F.T. (Frederick Theodore), 1929-
Financial crisis.

Bibliography: p.
Includes indexes.
1. International finance. 2. Loans, Foreign.
3. Business cycles. I. Title.
HG 3881.H268 1985 332'.042 85-12142
ISBN 0-275-90207-2 (alk paper)

Copyright © 1985 by Praeger Publishers

All rights reserved. No portion of this book may be reproduced, by any process or technique, without the express written consent of the publisher.

Library of Congress Catalog Card Number: 85-12142
ISBN: 0-275-90207-2

First published in 1985

Praeger Publishers, 521 Fifth Avenue, New York, NY 10175
A division of Greenwood Press, Inc.

Printed in the United States of America

The paper used in this book complies with the Permanent Paper Standards issued by the National Information Standards Organization (Z39.48-1984)

10 9 8 7 6 5 4 3 2

Contents

1

Introduction to Causes

A severe worldwide financial crisis is building and will culmunate in intervention by central banks in 1986 or 1987. It is probable that coordinated actions taken by governments of creditor nations will prevent a deep economic depression from occurring. Instead, the process of saving the capital of depositors in private banks, overlaid with a normal business cycle, will result in a severe recession during 1986–87.

The purpose of this book is to provide the framework for a solution to the financial crisis. If too much time is taken by the financial community in coming to the realization that a *global plan* is required instead of merely individual country rescue missions and then more time is taken to determine what specific actions must be taken, the 1986–87 recession could turn into a major depression.

Among the creditor nations, the United States is the country with the highest level of loan exposure in developing countries and the lowest level of reserves against bad debts. It is also the country purporting that (1) growth in the 1980s will permit borrowers to generate needed foreign exchange to service debt and (2) only country-by-country arrangements are needed. Parallel to making these declarations, the huge American budget deficits are making it more difficult for debtor countries to honor their obligations because of the resulting high real interest rates.

The first chapter deals with the underlying causes for the financial crisis currently developing.

SUMMARY OF THE CAUSES

The Rise in Crude Oil Prices

Chapter 4 covers this cause in detail. Briefly, however, in October 1973 OPEC decided on a 233% increase in price (production-weighted average prices). By end-1978 crude oil prices were 281% higher than in mid-1973. But the net oil importing nations had made significant adjustments. Global trade and the international financial infrastructure were recycling the petrodollars with acceptable efficiency. Governments were accelerating the development of resources that would generate hard currency, although painful mistakes were being made in the choice of projects. Wasteful energy practices were being eliminated, and the innovators were starting to search for petroleum substitutes. A few countries were overborrowed, but the likelihood that the 1973–78 changes in the cost of energy would cause an economic disaster was low.

Then in January 1979 the Iranian revolution removed the Shah, and this also eliminated a counterforce to radicals in OPEC. The 5.439 million barrels per day (b/d) produced by Iran before the Shah's departure became a 1.316 million b/d average in 1981. In addition, Iraq's 3.449 million b/d average in 1979 was reduced to 897,400 b/d in 1981 as a result of the war it initiated with Iran. The sudden loss of supply during 1979–81 contributed to OPEC's raising the price of crude oil per barrel as shown below (in U.S. dollars; OPEC posted prices weighted by average production):

1973	*1974–78*	*1979*	*1980*	*1981*	*1982–83*	*1984*
3.39	11.84	18.67	30.87	34.51	31.38	28.30

This dramatic rise in petroleum prices was apparently a turning point in the economic prospects of most net oil importing countries. In combination with American monetary policy and the rise in interest rates discussed later in this chapter, development of resources slowed and job formation fell behind the number of new entrants into the work force. Borrowing to cover current account deficits increased sharply. Also, the pattern of nonloan capital flows (equity investment) changed because private companies were less profitable and confidence in the future of many countries waned.

International banks competed for the surpluses of petrodollars created in oil exporting countries by offering attractive rates for deposits. This forced the banks to seek interest and fees on loans that would cover the relatively high cost of funds. Developing countries were targets for these credits. Unfortunately, the foreign exchange obtained by these countries from foreign borrowing paid increasingly for consumables (oil, food, and interest on past loans). Not enough went into gross fixed assets that add jobs and productive capacity for exports and for import substitution. This application of borrowed funds will play a major role in the need for a global solution to the financial crisis.

By the time oil prices started to fall in 1982, the damage had been done. Annual debt service in many countries grew beyond their capacity to generate foreign exchange, especially in a decelerating world economy (see Chapter 3). Formal rescheduling of previously rescheduled debt is taking place, and rollover loans are a common means of avoiding the necessity to reschedule.

By 1986 de facto defaults will grow in number. Even with the standard International Monetary Fund (IMF) adjustment program to limit imports in troubled countries and to regain export momentum, privately owned banks will be opting not to meet their needs whenever circumstances permit. World demand for soft loans will greatly exceed the funds available from the IMF and similar institutional sources. Depositors of some banks heavily committed in developing countries, especially the professionals with large organizations, are beginning to realize that a substantial number of assets in the form of loans to sovereign nations are not worth the stated amount. If no steps are taken to retain depositor confidence, substantial withdrawals could lead to a financial panic. This must be avoided by implementing one or a combination of the solutions presented in Chapters 6 and 7.

Attitudes and Expectations

Attitudes developed in the three decades before the 1980s that now play a role in today's fiscal budget deficits. Expectations rose and voters elected those politicians who promised greater economic security and increased access to social services. These are considered rights (referred to as "entitlements" in this book) in most advanced countries.

In less developed countries (LDCs), efficient worldwide communications enable citizens to compare their benefits and services with those of people in countries similar to their own. Pressure mounts in a democratic system to offer services that, however much needed, cannot be funded from normal revenues. Even authoritarian governments are attempting to provide benefits to minimize public dissent.

Nearly everyone has gained free time (shorter work weeks, longer vacations, more holidays, and compensation during layoffs). The legislative framework makes major demands on employers in the form of direct costs, red tape, time lost to litigation, and so on. Government is expected to produce benefits, and one tangible result is budget deficits. Another result is the weakening of the educational system as it competes for funds within these more limited budgets. In addition, huge bureaucracies have grown to administer and enforce entitlements.

Solutions to providing the required public revenue include:

1. Money supply is increased, which, in excess, feeds inflation and contributes to a devaluing currency.
2. Debt instruments are sold to domestic and foreign buyers, thereby potentially competing with private borrowers and producing higher interest rates and tight credit conditions. Alternatively, the government signs loan contracts with domestic and foreign lenders.
3. The negative effects of budget deficits are ignored. Inflation is dampened by a restrictive monetary policy, and higher interest rates result from the demand for money.
4. Taxes are raised. Legislation tends to target (a) old wealth that is depletable; (b) successful individuals, thereby potentially discouraging risk taking to generate new wealth or advance one's career through innovations in large organizations; and (c) companies, consequently diverting pretax profit from job creation and from distribution of earnings to shareholders who provide new capital for development.

Miscellaneous other sources of revenue are used. State-owned companies, such as petroleum operations, can generate income. Usually, however, these organizations are incurring losses and adding to the deficit. The key point is that, when funding of entitlements exceeds a government's prudent revenue-generating capacity, the probability is that politicians will turn to solutions harmful to the economy. The socioeconomic conditions and huge budget deficits at the close of 1984 suggest that this has indeed occurred. Extreme commitment to entitlements and interest due on borrowed funds is a major cause of the structurally weak conditions.

Politicians reflect public attitude. People want entitlements and generally do not care about the fiscal principles involved. Taxing the "rich" and "big business" and expanding the local currency debt "that we owe to ourselves" are perceived as the means of improving or maintaining benefits already received. Few countries (Switzerland and Taiwan–ROC are examples of exceptions) have had the discipline to insist on an equilibrium between entitlements offered and revenues received.

In many countries budget deficits have become such a financial burden that they limit a government's capacity to fight inflation, sluggish growth, and high interest rates. In some cases, such as the United States, social security programs are in deep financial trouble and future obligations are unfunded.

Hire/fire/overtime/layoff flexibility has been lost as a result of labor legislation that assures the entitlements of employees. In the 1970s employers were confronted with absenteeism, uneven worker behavior aimed at getting termination benefits, demands for self-management, strikes about sociopolitical issues, and sabotage to facilities. The quality of products and services declined in many countries because of worker alienation and indifference.

Management failed to respond with techniques to restore worker motivation and loyalty to the company, although some progress has occurred in the 1980s. In the years leading to the financial crisis, productivity suffered. Investment in labor-saving equipment to remain competitive in international markets was resisted because of unemployment. Attitudes of employees that are less understandable include refusing to (1) move from one work station to another, (2) learn to operate more-advanced machines, (3) change their skills as technology made them obsolete, and (4) move to another location where jobs were more plentiful. The Japanese recognized the problems elsewhere in the world broadly grouped under management of entitlements and seized the opportunity to gain market share.

Population Growth and Public Policy

Huge numbers of people have compounded the entitlements problem. The situation is further complicated by:

1. Migration toward the cities. The deterioration of facilities, their use well beyond designed capacity, and the

need for expanded sanitary facilities, education, housing, and other infrastructure contribute to budget deficits.

2. Reduced self-sufficiency in food. Encroachment on agricultural land by cities and structures (needed for electricity, highways, and so forth), the loss of farm labor, and inadequate mechanization of farming practices are decreasing agricultural output at a time when it is necessary to expand that capacity.

3. Pollution. The quality of life is being reduced by air, soil, sound, and water pollution. Private enterprise, as a result of control regulations, is diverting capital from job-creating expansion to prevention devices.

4. Mobility of people. Those with sought-after professions are leaving countries where conditions become unacceptable. Guest workers are returning home in many cases, but people with training and experience in advanced fields that would increase exports and help service foreign debt are avoiding troubled counties.

The need to mechanize and retain cost competitiveness and quality standards in international markets has been mentioned. Advanced countries are innovating and implementing new ideas rapidly, even in such traditional industries as automobiles, steel, and textiles. Developing countries are responding by adding modern facilities in priority operations. This limits job formation, upgrades skills that make people employable, and creates social burdens (unemployment, new educational needs, and security measures to control the jobless).

One solution commonly being applied is greater emphasis on agriculture as a source of employment. The objectives are to draw some people away from the cities, lessen dependency on capital- and energy-intensive industry, reduce food imports, and create jobs for individuals with few skills. Surplus agricultural output, when it develops, could earn hard currency. Theoretically, the solution is feasible in the long-range future if net population growth slows significantly. However, for many years cities will be inundated with masses of jobless people, living in slums characterized by crime, pollution, malnutrition, and violence. Governments will be using scarce resources to cope with these conditions. Serious riots will necessitate use of military forces and the training of troops in crowd control.

Such nations as India, Indonesia, Mexico, and Nigeria are being pulled into depressed socioeconomic conditions by the drag of millions of hopelessly poor people. In many countries during the 1970s, the rate of real economic growth outpaced the annual percentage of net population growth, but wealth remained concentrated in the upper 10% of the people. Investments prospered while inflation often reduced the gains in real income for workers. Corruption, direct and indirect (for example, channeling priority projects to family and friends), diverted wealth to the elite. This is one of the reasons why funds borrowed abroad did not go into projects that generated foreign exchange to service the payment obligations incurred.

The 1980s have been much less prosperous than the 1970s for nearly every country. IMF adjustment programs abound. Few people have the skills to participate in modern expanding industries. As a result, the unemployable underclass grew to present proportions. Psychologically, those who have moved to new locations seeking security and work are removed from their culture and the comfort of their traditions. For many, even if a job is found, an alien routine is involved. Personality changes occur that, if a large number of people is involved, have historically led to important adjustments in social structure. The spending to decrease the possibility of revolution, terrorism, and other avenues of violence are part of the financial crisis.

Currently, most developing economies are curtailing imports and reducing budget deficits. Those burdened with a net population growth rate of over 1% are experiencing great human suffering. Furthermore, their future looks terrible. For most of these countries, nearly half of the total population is under 15 years old. Idleness undermines family planning programs. As years pass, undernourished and frustrated people will dominate populations. Law and order will be under siege during the remainder of the century, regardless of actions by creditor nations to prevent collapse of the financial system. Personal security will become a paramount issue for the employed in the 1990s.

Budget Deficits and Interest Rates in the United States

The tables below indicate what has happened to American interest rates, budget deficits, and increases in money supply in recent years.

	1965	*1970*	*1975*	*1980*
Government Long-Term Bond Yield	4.27%	6.86%	8.19%	11.39%
Federal Budget Deficit (US$ billion)	1.60	11.38	75.40	68.72
Increase in M_1 Over Previous Year	4.8%	4.3%	5.5%	5.3%

	1981	1982	1983	1984
Government Long-Term Bond Yield	13.72%	12.92%	11.34%	12.72%
Federal Budget Deficit (US$ billion)	72.62	130.72	190.41	180.55
Increase in M_1 Over Previous Year	5.5%	5.6%	6.9%	7.8%

At the June 1984 Economic Summit, then-Treasury Department Secretary Donald T. Regan claimed that the budget deficits had nothing to do with interest rates in the United States. The statement was greeted with a range of replies by his peers from "simpleton position" to "patent nonsense." It is clear that money supply did not increase relative to need in the 1980s. When the government competes with private lending requirements as intensively as shown in the tables, a constant upward pressure on rates will result.

Real interest rates have become a major issue. The debtor countries believe that they should not pay the nominal rate but only the rate after subtracting inflation. The results for the same years shown in the above tables are as follows:

	1965	1970	1975	1980
Government Long-Term Bond Yield	4.27%	6.86%	8.19%	11.39%
Consumer Price Index Change	1.74	5.87	9.17	13.49
Real Interest Rate	2.53%	0.99%	-0.98%	-2.10%

	1981	1982	1983	1984
Government Long-Term Bond Yield	13.72%	12.92%	11.34%	12.72%
Consumer Price Index Change	10.40	6.07	3.25	5.44
Real Interest Rate	3.32%	6.86%	8.09%	7.28%

The impact of federal, state, and local government borrowing is seen in the real interest rates. The cost to debtor nations is immense because almost all of the loans approved in the 1980s involve a spread over the London Interbank Offered Rate (LIBOR) or the American prime rate. An upward move in either base rate represents millions of U.S. dollars to borrower. Friction escalated in 1984 when the American prime rate was raised to 13% immediately following the Cartegena (Colombia) meeting of Latin American debtors. The feeling of exploitation by bankers, advanced country governments, and the international financial agencies is growing. However, the most-frequent criticism is that the lack of fiscal discipline in the United States is causing misery and death in less developed countries.

An examination of "Reagonomics" is beyond the scope of this book. However, the concluding section of Chapter 5 discusses the Reagan administration's role in the financial crisis.

Motivations to Implement Solutions

Five factors indicate that a depression, if not avoided by some form of coordinated multigovernment intervention in the financial crisis, could be as severe as that of the 1930s, or worse.

1. Expectations of people in the mainstream of economies have reached relatively high levels. The contrast with a sudden deep decline in standard of living will have lasting psychological consequences, especially for the younger generation.
2. Interdependence of economic systems has increased, particularly in the process of investment and trade to pay for debt service, energy, and food. A sharp contraction in trade will mean unprecedented adjustments, as nations began to see in 1983–84.
3. The evolution of two superpowers with opposing ideologies and highly destructive military systems will lead to confrontation on a series of issues, as social conditions deteriorate and as both East and West cope with internal stress. The potential for war probably increases in a depression.
4. Country populations are much greater than in the 1930s. The financial resources to provide basic necessities for the increased number of people will not be proportionately adequate. As a result, the propensity to revert to crime and violence instead of submissive acceptance of conditions is greater.
5. The probability of stagflation instead of deflation is high for a depression because of (a) the tendency for public spending to greatly exceed revenues and (b) the possibility that a large volume of U.S. dollars will be converted to metals and other currencies in the process of rescuing American banks, thereby devaluing the U.S. dollar and increasing the cost of imported goods and services.

First Motivation

Elaborating on the five motivations to intervene now and reduce the probability of depression, only a small percentage of people remember the 1930s. Post–World War II generations living in advanced economies have come to expect the system to provide for them. Although young people often criticize the values of "big business" and "corrupt politicians," most of them accept help from these sources. As they mature, these people are absorbed into the establishment.

Generally, the populations of advanced countries are not prepared for the insecurity, hunger, and frustration common in developing countries. The tendency for many, perhaps 25% of the population according to psychiatrists, would be to strike at the system through spontaneous riots, organized nonviolent movements for fundamental change, illegal activities ("everybody's doing it"), and a few guerrilla movements. Groups citing various ideologies would frequently be guises for banditry and looting. Passive acceptance, compliance with laws, and patience until better times would be the reaction of the majority, about 75%. They would support repression of dissidents. Nevertheless, the dissident 25% would cause a violent period in the late 1980s.

Second Motivation

Export promotion, mass tourism, expanded sale of expertise and placement of expatriate workers has become a primary goal because of need for hard currency and the desire to meet obligations to creditors. The present level of dependence on trade with other nations did not exist in the 1930s. Communications and transportation facilities are now significantly better, and freedom to move across borders has improved. Countries like Brazil, Nigeria, and the Philippines, which are desperately seeking to build hard currency sources while limiting purchases, will find increasing resistance to one-way traffic. The turning point in global capacity to buy came in 1979–80, as mentioned, and the decline would be precipitous after 1985 without the intervention detailed in Chapter 6.

Third Motivation

World War III is not expected, regardless of financial circumstances. The two superpowers will posture and maneuver for strategic gains even while they suffer socioeconomic hardships within their borders. A nuclear holocaust is not predicted to result if a deep depression develops, but fear and tension not present in the 1930s would persist throughout the period of economic troubles in the West. Regional wars, undertaken by local nations but often promoted by superpowers, would be a ploy to divert attention from internal conditions.

One possibility is Soviet domination (not occupation) of Western Europe as a result of the following factors:

1. Conflicts within NATO on nuclear armament arise from such influences as peace movements and arbitrary American political and military decisions that cause alienation and weaken ties between the United States and many European countries.
2. American preoccupation with the financial crisis—and consequent socioeconomic problems at home—limit spending on the country's armed forces and reduce capacity to respond to Soviet attempts to gain influence in Western Europe.
3. The Kremlin opts for an aggressive, prestige-building trade campaign with depressed Western European economies, citing a need for greater agricultural and industrial interdependence.
4. The natural gas flowing from the USSR to Europe through the new pipeline creates only minimal energy dependency but plays a role in weakening resolve to resist Soviet influence.
5. Fragile governments hold power for short periods as economic conditions deteriorate, and factions align with the Soviet Union to lengthen their tenure in office.

Even if "Finlandization" does not occur in Europe, most people would be worried about the quality of American leadership, America's will to defend Europe, and the possibility of World War III. The extreme left and right would attempt to build antigovernment sentiments throughout the world, and professional terrorist operations would work in concert with natural feelings of resentment. Individual insecurity would be greater than in the 1930s.

Fourth Motivation

Because of large populations, most governments would not be able to adequately prevent a large portion of their people from enduring extreme poverty and malnutrition. Urban densities would add to the misery. Advanced countries would attempt public works programs, feeding stations, and barracks-style housing in idle buildings.

Developing countries would have to ignore portions of their population in any program of providing basic necessities because equal distribution of limited amounts of food, shelter, and medical supplies would mean disaster for everyone. Living conditions in the 1930s were bad, but research indicates that greater numbers of people would make conditions at the end of this decade relatively worse, despite improvements in standards since that time.

Fifth Motivation

Double-digit inflation is probable if a depression occurs. However, hyperinflation such as the Germans experienced in 1923 is not a possibility. Saving the depositors of banks with an infusion of cash through solutions suggested in this book would create some excess liquidity, but huge budget deficits and consequent public borrowing would absorb most of the funds. Amounts of foreign debt exposure are large in some countries, particularly in the United States, but recommended solutions involve phased payments to the banks, not single payments. As a result, stagflation would be contained to less than 20% in most countries.

The scenario in which hyperinflation is caused by the +US$750 billion in banks abroad coming back to the United States in a wave of waning confidence in the country is also not a possibility. Research indicates firm resolve on the part of central banks to maintain the stability of the U.S. dollar because it is the mechanism for world trade. Without this medium of payment, a period of depression would surely occur because of the financial obstruction to international commerce. However, substantial movement out of the U.S. dollar would take place during an American banking crisis, and the exchange rate would fall from present heights to levels such as those seen in the last half of 1978 (for instance, US$1 = DM1.70). Imported goods and services would increase in cost. In combination with liquidity created by rescuing the banks and public spending to soften the impact of a depressed economy, the American inflation rate would approximate 15%, and the prime interest rate would be about 20% because the government would be borrowing immense amounts of money.

THE TIMING FOR CULMINATION OF THE CRISIS

The paragraphs below are written as a concise scenario of what will occur in the coming months. Completion of editing took place at end-March 1985 and the possibility of a banking system collapse was not perceived by most government decision makers.

The Financial Crisis

The business downturn that took place in 1986–87 started in the United States. After the November 1984 elections, attempts were begun to reduce the federal budget deficit and remove the primary cause of high real interest rates. Government spending at the federal level is nearly 25% of gross national product. Major cuts in expenditures were not made, and higher taxes were not legislated. Large additions to money supply were intended to lower interest rates and to prevent economic deceleration during 1985. Nevertheless, saturation of consumer and industrial capacity to buy developed and the economy slowed.

Europe and Japan retained most of their economic momentum in 1985, but they entered 1986 with the prospects of deceleration because of lower levels of demand in the United States and no compensating markets in the developing countries due to IMF adjustment programs and self-induced austerity plans to cope with financial problems. Hence, business began to slow significantly and demand for commodities—including crude oil—decreased. Downward pressures on prices of these commodities mounted and the foreign exchange generation of nations with large foreign debts declined.

In late 1985 the number of moratoriums, reschedulings of previously rescheduled debt, and countries with interest arrears grew. It was apparent that the pace of the world economy would not permit prompt interest payments and that principal payments were impossible. Brazil had a new president in March 1985. He was given a grace period to organize his government, but he died before his inauguration; this extended the grace period because of the need for President José Sarney to consolidate his hold on power. Mexico was negotiating its second IMF adjustment program to begin in December 1985, and the fall in crude oil prices made it clear that interest payments would be a problem that could not be solved by a fundamental restructuring of the country's debt profile. Latin American countries were variously asking for interest rates based on the cost of money (no margin for overhead and profits) or on real interest rates to discount the impact of American budget deficits.

In the first months of 1986, the realities for American

banks became apparent. Arrears on interest payments by many foreign borrowers meant acknowledging that these loans were no longer assets. The number of banks reaching bankruptcy when this adjustment was made (many of their domestic loans would be in default as well as international loans) was sufficiently great that Congress had to act quickly to avoid a bank panic. The Federal Deposit Insurance Corporation (FDIC) was appropriated huge sums to protect depositors, and action was taken to prevent collapse of the banking system in FY1987. End of scenario.

The purpose of this book is to offer suggestions on what actions should be taken. Mistakes are made in a crisis, and it is better to have a contingency plan that minimizes the probability of serious mistakes.

REFERENCES

FORELEND. Business Environment Risk Information S.A., 1985–I.

1983 World Debt Tables. International Bank for Reconstruction and Development, 1984.

International Financial Statistics Yearbook 1983, June 1983, June 1984, and January 1985. International Monetary Fund.

2

Brief Review of Business Cycle Theory

KONDRATIEFF'S LONG WAVES

The concepts of Nikolai Kondratieff's (a nineteenth-century Russian economist) long waves of economic expansion and contraction were first given broad recognition in the 1920s. The years involved in his original work were the first two waves identified below. The years given for the third wave are generally accepted by economists who work using this concept. A fourth wave is added by the author to update the theory. Even with optimal and timely decisions taken to resolve the impending financial crisis, a period of adjustment to new conditions will result.

1.	1792–1850	Expansion	1792–1815	23 years
	58 years	Contraction	1815–1850	35 years
2.	1850–96	Expansion	1850–73	23 years
	46 years	Contraction	1873–96	23 years
3.	1896–1940	Expansion	1896–1920	24 years
	44 years	Contraction	1920–40	20 years
4.	1940–88	Expansion	1940–69	29 years
	48 years	Contraction	1969–88	19 years

The four waves over a 196-year period average 49 years (expansion, 24.75 years; contraction, 24.25 years). Selection of 1969 as the culmination of the expansion period in the current wave is compatible with the choices of 1815, 1873, and 1920. In each contraction portion of a long wave, there are brief periods of recovery from modest recessions. Nevertheless, a relatively sustained downturn took place after these faltering attempts at regaining expansion momentum. In each of the four years at the end of an expansion period, a sustained period of prosperity came to an end.

The 1969–88 contraction period has not yet involved a period of depression. Some developing countries have incurred sustained periods of negative growth associated with austerity programs designed to meet debt service payments. However, average conditions are far better than those of the previous contraction period. The mechanisms and organizations are in place to avoid extremely poor economic conditions.

SHORTER CYCLES

The Juglar cycle (Clement Juglar, a nineteenth-century French physician) averaged eight years during the 1825–1929 period. In the post-World War II period, the recessions [A recession is defined as two successive quarters in which real gross national product declines. The "pauses" in 1960–61 and 1966–67 did not conform to this definition.] before the 1973 oil price increase occurred in 1948–49, 1957–58, and 1969–71. These cycles averaged almost eleven years, but four of Juglar's cycles were similar in length. The two recessions that occurred in recent years, 1974–75 and 1981–83, have been induced by causes associated with the 918% rise in crude oil prices from late 1973 to mid-1981.

The magnitude of the crude oil price increases produced a severe shock to the world's macroeconomic system. The combined results in advanced and developing countries conform with models for the exogenous factor theory (defined as the alternative consequences of such extraordinary events as a major war, far-reaching innovation, and global crop failure). Professor Hyman Minsky (Chicago-born, contemporary American economist) conceived alternatives for the aftermath of exceptional events that assists in the interpretation of current developments. This concept would lead to the conclusion that a serious depression will begin in 1987.

The socioeconomic conditions in the 1980s are not generally similar to the periods in which other causal theories were conceived. The efforts by advanced countries to escape the entrapment caused by the high price of oil imports led to an emphasis on technology and innovation to develop products that require minimal inputs of energy and unskilled labor. This upgrading of employable personnel has created an underclass of people who cannot find jobs and who are consequently a drain on government budgets. If industries are to remain competitive in world markets, they must continually automate and upgrade the production process. This is inconsistent with high population growth rates and high unemployment levels, but the need for convertible currency from exports forces the use of modern equipment in most cases.

THE INVESTMENT MULTIPLIER AND THE CONSUMPTION ACCELERATOR

References are made to the relationship between investment, consumption, and growth. Any new expenditure (for instance, an office building or factory) generates several times as much income as the initial expenditure. Those who are paid will spend a major portion of what they receive, and this will become income for others, who in turn spend most of what they receive, and so on. Every new investment generates an impact called the "investment multiplier" and provides impetus for expansion. Consumer demand, stimulated by income from investment, often in turn requires new production facilities. This result is known as the "consumption accelerator." An increase in national income normally stimulates investment.

The strength of the upward cyclical movement depends on the degree of income multiplication in a country and on subsequent increases in investment. The use of consumer credit, including low-cost mortgages, as a means of increasing consumption has added upward pressure in countries where interest rates are not judged to be too high. Strong downward pressures occur when this credit becomes tight or too expensive.

A point in the cycle is eventually reached at which land, labor, and capital are being fully utilized. In the 1980s unused facilities and untrained people are available, but they are not competitive in today's markets and therefore become liabilities instead of assets. Advanced technology involves investment in software, new concepts, and specialized equipment. Because there is much less spending for construction, heavy equipment, and materials, people with minimal skills are required to a much smaller degree. The consequences are (1) that multiplication of investment is relatively small when compared to past decades and (2) that the consumption accelerator is minimal.

The outlook for return on investment periodically turns unfavorable due to (1) saturation of demand, (2) increased cost of money, plant, and equipment, (3) or a sudden shock to the economy, such as high energy costs. In the case of investment that is dependent on government spending, if budget deficits are characteristic in times of expansion, these deficits will limit a nation's capacity to stimulate the economy during periods of contraction. With no increase in employment and no rise in consumer demand, operation of the consumption accelerator ceases. Decreasing demand and a decline in the amount of new capital being generated slow investment markedly, and workers are laid off. Thus, the descriptive terms become the "investment and consumption decelerators."

The slope of the decline depends on the composition of the economy and on the way its population allocates its income between consumption and savings. This choice affects both the levels of consumer demand and capital investment. In the United States savings as a percent of disposable income was extremely low at 4.9% during 1983; individuals opted to use their earnings for goods and services rather than allocate large portions to savings. This strengthens the expansion phase of the business cycle. When confidence starts to fade and personal reserves are low, Americans tend to increase savings; this decelerates demand and builds inventories. Japanese have a consistently high level of savings (over 20%), and this moderates the amplitude of a cycle. Demand is more consistent, and capital is available for equity investment.

The lower limit of a business cycle is difficult to predict, but it is established when forces permit the investment multiplier and consumption accelerator to operate. Countries that are reducing government investment and are discouraging consumption through austerity programs that are scheduled for several years (because of structural budget and current account deficits) are creating deep troughs in the business cycle.

The occurrence of time lags—delays between a decision and its effect—is a factor in the process. This is illustrated by the two recessions that followed many months after a major increase in oil prices. By anticipating the impact of developments and making suitable adjustments, it is possible to minimize the amplitude of the cycle. Early action to defuse the financial crisis is an example. Lags will occur between the decision to act and the realization of the solution design, and this lag could create a deep trough in the 1986–87 recession and lengthen it in 1988.

THE THEORY AND CURRENT CONDITIONS

The overriding factor is underutilized industrial capacity. For example, the United States was operating at 81% of installed capacity at end-1984 despite the 6.8% real growth during the year. Investment is being confined to cost-cutting rationalization (which usually means fewer jobs), quality-creating mechanization, and successful high technology businesses that require high level of skills. Demand, which would raise the operating rate, is being constrained by the contraction in world trade. The consumer-led period of prosperity during 1983–85 masks some fundamentals. These include:

1. Loans to Argentina, Brazil, Mexico, and Venezuela listed as assets on the books of the ten largest American banks at end-1983 represented 116% of their equity capital.
2. The United States federal budget deficit averaged US$165.5 billion per year during 1983–85. This means that prosperity was fabricated out of borrowed money. Any correction will convert the consumption accelerator to a decelerator.
3. Real interest rates averaged an extraordinary 7.7% during 1983–85. The high cost of money could be tolerated only by businesses with exceptional rates of return or by parties gaining from mergers. Conditions discouraged the progress possible with broad application of the investment multiplier.

Most countries are overborrowed as a result of the exogenous event (crude oil price escalation). The option of funding programs to stimulate real growth through foreign loans has been lost because (1) petrodollar recycling has decelerated, (2) liquidity from repayments of principal and interest is minimal because of involuntary rollovers and rescheduling, and (3) private bank efforts to put their loan portfolio into a reasonable risk exposure profile. Each of these factors limits the flow of fresh monies to distressed countries. Inability to pay for imports is choking economies. The result is a centripetal force (inward) in both advanced and developing countries leading to protectionism and sharply reduced international markets.

Currently, major borrowers (countries) are investing less and less in their industrial infrastructure at a time when debt service requires expansion. Principal and interest payments are being rescheduled for future periods when the countries will be even less able to pay lenders than at the present time because of physical limits on volume feasible to ship (the condition of rolling stock, port facilities, and transportation networks has deteriorated badly) and because of the growing magnitude of the debt. Loss of order in the process of economic contraction could come from indecisive handling of bank failures, arbitrary moratoriums, and joint debtor actions.

REFERENCES

Burns, Arthur F., and Wesley C. Mitchell. *Measuring Business Cycles,* 1946.

Hansen, A.H. *Business Cycles and National Income,* 1964.

Kindleberger, Charles P. *Maias, Panics and Crashes,* 1978.

Schumpeter, Joseph A. *Business Cycles: A Theoretical, Historical, and Statistical Analysis of the Capitalist Process,* two volumes, 1939.

3

The Financial Condition of Countries in 1985

This chapter consists of two parts: first, observations are made on governmental decisions in the United States during 1985 and their general impact on economic conditions; second, twenty important countries are analyzed, and forecasts for the 1980s are given based on conditions that are partly the result of the American decisions.

THE 1986–87 RECESSION—THE AMERICAN TRIGGER

The United States had a US$101.6 billion current account deficit in 1984, the largest amount in world history. Yet, the balance of payments was slightly positive. Overall, the U.S. dollars leaving the country to pay for imported goods and services (plus unrequited transfers) returned to the United States in the capital account. This recycling of U.S. dollars depends on the following criteria:

1. The United States is a safe place; convertibility and repatriation of capital and earnings is assured.
2. The real interest rate is comparable or superior to alternative investments.
3. The exchange rate risk is minimal; the tendency of the U.S. dollar is to strengthen rather than weaken against other currencies.
4. Foreign parties have funds to invest in U.S. dollar securities and American property. Obligations do not fully

consume capital, nor are alternatives in other currencies more attractive than options in the United States.

The exchange rate of most currencies against the U.S. dollar reached extraordinarily low levels in early 1985 before the corrections later in the year. Interest rates began to ease in the second quarter with a surge of money supply to combat economic deceleration. With little upward movement in the American inflation rate, U.S. dollar securities were earning lower real interest rates. As the U.S. dollar weakened, (1) imports became costlier, (2) upward pressures on prices were greater, and (3) consumer and industrial capacity to buy diminished. The average forecast for real economic growth in the United States during 1985 changed to 2.4% from 3.8%.

A consensus developed in the first half of 1985 that the U.S. dollar was seriously overvalued. The moves begun in September 1985 by the United States and other countries to depreciate the U.S. dollar were needed to decrease both the huge current account deficits and the rapid accumulation of foreign debt by the American government. The turning point precipitating a financial crisis occurred in 1985 when the United States Congress (1) used inflated revenue estimates when calculating future fiscal year deficits, (2) failed to raise taxes to reduce the deficits that it acknowledged, (3) achieved no compromise on spending cuts within the defense/social programs issue, and (4) refused to deal with a crisis in agriculture, adding to the gravity of the banking crisis in 1986–87. Equally important, banks with loans to nations in arrears on interest payments were not forced to create reserves against the possibility of default on these loans, increasing the number of failures when they are valueless as an asset to offset depositor liabilities.

If the Americans had made significant progresss in reducing the federal budget deficit after the 1984 election, it is probable that the recession predicted for 1986–87 would be less severe. At the outset of 1985 it was necessary to decrease the FY1985 deficit (ending 30 September), not just debate the FY1986 deficit. The pivotal time was the third quarter of 1985 when government borrowing in money markets to close the fiscal year would either drive interest rates higher and encourage a recession or be accommodated by a strong rise in money supply and encourage inflation along with price escalation from a devaluing dollar. This situation had been created by the ideologists led by President Reagan and Defense Secretary Weinberger who prevailed over the pragmatists (Senator Dole, Chairman Volker, and others). Lobbyists battled for their budget lines successfully. Consequently, the government itself played a major role in creating the financial crisis.

THE FINANCIAL CONDITION OF TWENTY SELECTED COUNTRIES IN 1985

The analyses and forecasts of the twenty countries are given in alphabetical order. The author has created the four categories shown in Table 3–1 to identify their probable financial condition in the 1986–90 period.

TABLE3-1. Probable Financial Condition of Twenty Selected Countries during 1986-90

De Facto Default 4	Deteriorating Toward Crisis 3	Improving-- No Crisis 2	Strong Financial Condition 1
Argentina	Australia	Canada	Japan
Brazil	Colombia	France	Saudi Arabia
Mexico	Egypt	India	Taiwan (ROC)
Nigeria	Indonesia	Korea (South)	United Kingdom
Philippines	South Africa	Spain	
Venezuela			

Differences exist, of course, between countries within each of the four categories. Brazil, for example, has a diversified economy that will be resilient when the debt burden is relieved through solutions mentioned in this book or others devised later in the decade; the country is very likely to become prosperous in the 1990s. Australia has both the human and natural resources to rectify its financial problems; currently, the leadership is not in the political position to introduce the necessary stringent measures, and the Australian people do not think that it is necessary to endure austerity. In summary, there is another order within the four categories that becomes apparent when reading the following country analyses.

Argentina—4

The IMF US$19 billion package of loans and credits has only postponed the timing of default. The current inflation rate of 600% annually and pressures from organized labor for wage increases will perpetuate the economic crisis. Although President Alfonsín has retained personal popularity, he lacks the political strength needed to implement austerity policies.

Assessment of Quantitative Factors

Despite a drop in meat exports, the trade surplus reached an estimated US$3.4 billion in 1984, about the same as the 1983 surplus (US$3.7 billion). This surplus will rise to almost US$4.0 billion in 1985. Soybean production and grain exports hit record highs in 1984. Nevertheless, Argentina has experienced serious problems because of heavy interest repayment obligations that are in excess of the trade surplus. Regardless of multiyear rescheduling, the country will continually incur a current account deficit and require fresh monies for interest payments. The government banned repatriation of profits, dividends, and royalties in May 1984 to save foreign exchange reserves. Argentina's foreign debt is ±US$45 billion, excluding the additional loans of US$5.6 billion in the end-December 1984 refinancing package. With the help of last-minute pledges of US$500 million from the United States and US$100 million from Latin America, Argentina managed to pay US$850 million in interest due on 31 December 1984. The payment still left arrears of US$500 million in interest payments. Its budget deficit is approximately 10% of its GDP.

Assessment of Qualitative Factors

Argentina had expressed hostility toward IMF terms but has become more conciliatory in order to obtain cooperation from the international financial community. On 28 December 1984 the IMB approved a US$19 billion package of loans and credits at favorable terms. IMF loans total US$1.4 billion. Commercial banks will provide new loans of US$4.2 billion with interest at 1.625% over LIBOR. They also will extend for 10–12 years the repayment of US$13.4 billion that had been due by the end of 1985; the interest rate was 1.375 percentage points over LIBOR and three years without any principal due. Incredibly, the United States federal lending regulators upgraded the status of loans to Argentina from "substandard" to "other transfer risk," in recognition of the IMF package and the progress Argentina has made toward repaying interest after earlier threats of default. The country has no chance whatsoever of remaining current on interest without doing what it did in 1983: borrowing more money. At 1.25% over LIBOR (six months), or an average interest rate of 10.5%, the country will owe US$5.3 billion in interest alone. This sum will overwhelm the trade surplus, and another round of emergency negotiations will be necessary.

Sociopolitical and Business Forecast

The government faces a no-win situation. Hyperinflation averaged 583% in 1984 and cannot be reduced without sacrificing economic recovery and sociopolitical stability. Political opposition in Argentina is fragmented within labor unions and the Peronist party, but these factions uniformly reject austerity measures. The Confederación General del Trabajo has demanded real wage increases that are triple the amount conceded by the government. Alfonsín is holding on to the presidency against this opposition and against the military officers who are starting to regain a positive self-image. The military is angry over his dismissal of the army chief of staff and other top officers, military budget cuts, and his prosecution of military leaders for human rights violations. The president demonstrated his political acumen amid criticism of his administration's peace treaty with Chile to settle the Beagle Channel dispute; despite a boycott organized by the Peronists, a majority of the voters participated in the nonbinding plebiscite 25 November 1984 and approved the treaty. The president's personal popularity will wane during 1985–86; with growing unrest stemming from economic decline and exacerbated by a world recession, the military will overthrow the civilian government once again.

Australia—3

The 144% rise in foreign debt over the past four years has generated an alarming debt service burden that will place severe constraints on the country's current account performance and foreign exchange reserves. Payments for oil imports and debt service now take ±65% of foreign exchange earnings. Government or foreign bank guarantees should be required on loans to private parties toward the end of the forecast period.

Assessment of Quantitative Factors

Total foreign debt will reach about US$45 billion by year-end 1985, and will represent about 21% of GDP. The external debt statistics are particularly alarming because additions to capacity to generate foreign exchange have not kept pace with the rate of borrowing from abroad. The current account deficit is returning to disastrously high levels (revised to US$8,450 million in 1984 and ±US$9 billion in 1985). The invisibles deficit jumped over 36% last year and will continue rising. The trade account has moved back into deficit; domestic demand is pulling in consumer goods and industrial inputs faster than the growth of mineral and agricultural exports. Export manufacturing will not achieve sufficient competitiveness to make a major contribution to foreign exchange earnings. Foreign equity capital inflows continue to decline, and the overall balance of payments surplus is being eroded. Australia will have to borrow to fund current account deficits as of this year. This easily covers the frequently heavy outflows due to corporate debt repayments. Fiscal factors are improving, largely because dynamic recovery boosts revenues. The budget deficit will therefore drop to about 3.6% of GDP this year.

Assessment of Qualitative Factors

The negative factor will be debt restructuring required by foreign exchange problems after mid-1986. Most of the intangible factors affecting the country's ability and willingness to meet its foreign obligations will be strongly positive throughout the 1980s. Australia's financial and economic managers are competent; political interference and corruption are minimal. The terms and structure of new loans will be tightened, however, because of deteriorating quantitative fundamentals.

Sociopolitical and Business Forecast

Bob Hawke's reduced majority was partly attributable to invalid ballots caused by new voting procedures. Nevertheless, the longer term consequences include (1) a weakening of his position within the faction-ridden Australian Labor Party (ALP) and (2) an unexpected boost for Liberal Party leader Andrew Peacock. Hawke will have difficulty pushing through further changes in the inflationary national pay determination system. Belated austerity measures to cope with Australia's domestic and external financial problems in 1986–87 will produce labor unrest and political backlash. Peacock is therefore likely to win the 1987 elections and form the next government, possibly in coalition with the National Party of Australia (formerly the

National Country Party). Surging growth (real GDP ±6.2% in 1985) will fall back to ±3.0% this year. Agricultural output will decline from its postdrought boom, and the mining industry faces a period of stagnation. Inflation, which fell to 4.2% on the strength of one-time changes in the CPI, will be about 5% this year.

Brazil—4

Economic recovery is beginning, but the new civilian government will want to apply available funds to domestic growth and will reopen discussions with international lenders on terms for debt repayment. The Jose Sarney administration will have more legitimacy to implement economic changes, but the death of Tancredo Neves and uncertainty about the tenure of Sarney (early direct elections in 1986 are probable) makes increased foreign investment less likely. The key issues in the coming years will be foreign exchange generation and debt service performance in the next recession and the impact of severe austerity measures in this period on sociopolitical stability. Brazil's economic performance has exceeded expectations in 1983–84, and 1985 will be a good year. However, the following three years are going to be very difficult.

Assessment of Quantitative Factors

Declining oil prices, lower world interest rates, and increased trade permitted Brazil's economic performance in 1984 to exceed targets. Performance should also be good in 1985. The merchandise trade surplus will drop slightly this year from the 1984 high of US$12.5 billion due to saturation in some markets, inventory replenishment at home protectionist measures, and increased competition. The 1985 current account deficit will be just under US$3 billion, higher than the US$1,150 million in 1984 but well below the huge deficits of the 1980–83 period. Oil imports were down 14% in 1984 below the previous year's imports, representing a savings of about US$1.25 billion in foreign exchange. Unemployment began dropping in late 1984, and an increase in disposable income spurred domestic demand. Monetary expansion in 1984 was a very high 228%, contributing strongly to inflation.

Sociopolitical and Business Forecast

Political consensus in favor of the Sarney government is dissipating quickly in 1985. Sarney is a role model for the power structure that was displaced early in the year. His hold on the office of president is weak, and he will be persuaded to permit direct elections in 1986. Meanwhile, the parties will undergo restructuring and reorganization during 1985–86. Progress toward building domestic industry and creating jobs, policies likely to reduce social unrest, will be minimal in this transition period. Labor agitation will increase, as unions exercise rights denied them under the military. Economic recovery began in earnest during 1984, when GNP grew by 3.5% and industrial production rose by ±6.5%. The 1985 GNP growth target is 5% to 6%. Inflation will continue to hover in the ±200% range in 1985. The end-1983 to end-1984 rate was 208.8%. Continuing high interest rates will be a serious drag on domestic investment.

Canada—2

Some restructuring of U.S. dollar-dominated foreign debt to reduce average interest rates can be expected in the first half of 1985. Developments in the American economy will be reflected in Canada because the United States generates about one-fifth of Canadian GDP by taking up to 70% of its exports. The Progressive Conservative government's decision to strengthen cross-border ties will therefore have adverse political and economic consequences due to deficit cutting by Washington and recession in 1986–87. Stability is ensured through 1988 because of the breadth of Conservative support and the easing of Quebec separatism. Long-term growth prospects are only moderate because of weak markets for minerals and forest products, the backbone of the Canadian economy.

Assessment of Quantitative Factors

The loan profile is improved and budget deficits as a percentage of GDP have declined. The new conservative technocrats are sophisticated and competent; political interference is nil. Canada continues to benefit from favorable loan terms, although lender caution about specific projects is apparent. Terms of 0.050% over LIBOR for 8–10 years are common.

Sociopolitical and Business Forecast

The massive sweep of the Progressive Conservative Party will give Prime Minister Brian Mulroney wide latitude to implement his probusiness, "pay-as-you-go" domestic policies. Deficit-cutting measures will be extended. Opposition will be muted by both the current prosperity and the breadth of Mulroney's support. His moves to strengthen U.S.-Canadian relations will also be endorsed as long as the American economy engenders jobs and prosperity. However, economic nationalism remains a latent force. Constructive dialogues with Quebec will be aided by the Parti Québécois' recent turn toward economic pragmatism. The business environment will benefit from above average growth (3.0% in 1985 after 4.5% in 1984); inflation will be moderate but rising (±5.0%). The government's attempt to cut the FY1985/86 spending by US$3.2 billion will not succeed in reducing the deficit, which will rise from US$26.1 billion to US$28 billion. The prime rate is currently 11.75%, above the traditional one percentage point spread over U.S. rates.

Colombia—3

The financial situation is becoming rapidly worse, and solutions are at least two years away from having impact. The next years will be difficult for Colombia, with declining exports in 1986–87, little new credit, and foreign exchange shortages for repayments. Rescheduling will keep Colombia from defaulting until conditions improve later in the decade, but some interest payments will be delayed.

Assessment of Quantitative Factors

The seemingly endemic current account deficit is adding to external debt. Merchandise imports were severely restricted and declined 14%; exports rose 22%; but the preliminary current account deficit was US$1,375 million. With foreign exchange difficult to borrow and reserves covering 60 days of imports, Colombia has sold more gold; this accounts for part of the gain in exports. Capital flight is compounding the problem; an increase in crawling peg devaluations to 28% in 1984 has helped to slow flight of capital, although the peso remains overvalued. Coffee remains the major product, accounting for 52% of export earnings. The importance of coal exports will increase over the next five years due to the El Cerrejón project, but full-scale output will encounter falling energy prices in 1986. With new reserves discovered in the Llanos region, Colombia is approaching oil self-sufficiency for the first time since 1976. In the next five years, it will eliminate its US$200 million oil trade deficit; however, due to declining production in older fields, net oil exports are unlikely. Colombia has accumulated public foreign debt of US$10.8 billion in 1984 and private foreign debt of US$4.4 billion; this total means US$1,350 million in interest payments, or 27% of foreign exchange earnings.

Assessment of Qualitative Factors

Colombia has managed to honor all debt obligations. It is one of the few Latin American nations to make payments on principal (almost equal to interest payments). Without substantial new loans or rescheduling, however, Colombia will be unable to be current on its debt service when exports drop during the 1986–87 recession. Geographical proximity to extreme debtor nations has made it difficult to convince lenders to extend new credit. Nevertheless, the Inter-American Development Bank has offered to lend US$455 million for housing and electricity development, and the World Bank has said it might be willing to provide US$300 million for export production, in addition to 1984 loans of US$220 million. Colombia currently has no IMF loans.

Sociopolitical and Business Forecast

President Betancur continues his attacks on illegal drug operations. Some major traffickers have gone into exile, and relations with the United States have improved. However, drug traffic has been cut by only 5%–10%, and drug-related violence continues. Despite occasional skirmishes and some violence from small guerrilla groups that rejected the truces, the 28 May 1984 cease-fire with FARC and the 24 August 1984 cease-fire with M-19 will endure during the first stage. However, these one-year truces are not likely to be extended. Although the military has opposed Betancur, particularly his conciliation with the guerrillas, popular support for Betancur has been strong. GDP growth, ±2.0% for 1984, was led by agriculture, construction, mining, and oil production. Although it represented an improvement over 0.8% in 1983, economic growth still lagged behind the population's growth rate. Because of difficulties in attracting foreign capital and the need to reduce expenditures, the government has been able to implement only part of its US$21.4 billion national plan for 1983–86, thus delaying economic recovery indefinitely. Inflation has improved each year since 1981 and declined to 16% in 1984; prices will rise ±25% in 1985 due to accelerated devaluations. A high inflation rate, high unemployment, and wage controls have increased unrest. Legal activities in political mobilization by former guerrillas will increase organized protests.

Egypt—3

Egypt is bargaining for a substantial increase in American aid for 1986 and beyond to help compensate for falling oil prices and an expected decline in workers' remittances from abroad. Despite some increase in assistance and improved control over merchandise imports, sporadic shortages of foreign exchange will continue, and delays will occur on trade payments and debt service. The country's strategic value in the Middle East is always a dominant factor.

Assessment of Quantitative Factors

The downward trend in world oil consumption and prices will affect workers' remittances in addition to the Sumed Pipeline revenues, Suez Canal receipts, and petroleum export earnings. Many Egyptians working abroad are in Middle Eastern oil states. Workers' remittances amounted to a record US$3.4 billion in fiscal 1984 (July 1983–June 1984) but are expected to drop to below US$3 billion in 1985. Last year the current account deficit returned to ±US$1,050 million after the major drop in 1983 to US$785 million. In 1985 the deficit will be about the same as in 1984. Foreign exchange earnings from oil, about US$2.2 billion per year, have been maintained by increasing output. Production now averages 910,000 b/d compared with an average of 840,000 b/d during fiscal 1984 and 768,550 b/d in 1983. Rising domestic demand lessens the added amount available for export. The Suez Canal earned just under US$1 billion in fiscal 1984, and this income will be similar in 1985 because tolls have been raised an average of 3.7%, effective from 1 January 1985.

The government claims that it will be able to reduce the US$6.4 billion deficit in the fiscal 1985 budget through new revenues from the autumn 1984 tax package and gradual reduction of the subsidies on staple items, electricity, and petroleum. It is difficult to measure progress on subsidy reduction, however, since the government is very slow to release figures on actual expenditure. The exchange rate adjustments in December 1984 amount to a minidevaluation of the Egyptian pound for certain transactions (workers' remittances, tourism, and imports) and recognize the strength of the blackmarket exchange rate in October-November, when an acute shortage of foreign exchange occurred. The complicated multiple exchange rate system is causing pressure for currency reform. External public debt is presently about US$21 billion, with debt service of US$2.5 billion and a debt service ratio above 22%.

Assessment of Qualitative Factors

Egypt is seeking a major increase in aid from the United States for 1986. It will request US$3.15 billion, to consist of US$250 million under the PL-480 grain import program. For 1985 Egypt is receiving a total of ±US$2.2 billion from the United States, all in grant form for the first time. America's strong support is of vital importance in view of the deteriorating prospects for foreign exchange earnings. Japan's latest annual aid package totals US$208 million, divided among seven development projects. It will contain a higher proportion of grants than before. The World Bank is providing US$150–200 million for a scheme to introduce modern farm machinery in agricultural operations. The government is determined to proceed with the first part of its eight-station nuclear power program, which may be partially financed by a US$250 million loan form the United States' Export-Import Bank.

Sociopolitical and Business Forecast

President Hosni Mubarak's foreign policy gains will increase his authority at home. Egypt has resumed its place in the Islamic Conference, diplomatic ties have been restored with Jordan, and relations with Israel appear to be improving. However, these events will also rouse radicals firmly opposed to the regime's cautious policies. The reinstatement of Pope Chenouda III is part of an effort to lessen religious strife. Unrest is currently focused on price rises rather than religious differences. Inflation is presently in a range of 20% to 30%, with real GDP growth at about 7%. Business activity is quite strong in areas related to petroleum and construction (projects tied to aid are the key factors).

France—2

A bulge in debt service payments after 1985 will coincide with a renewed contraction of international trade, exacerbating France's financial problems. By the end of the forecast period the rating will have improved under the probable combination of a stable center-right government that makes sound financial management a top priority and international expansion that cuts the trade deficit.

Assessment of Quantitative Factors

Despite restructuring in 1984 and 1985 to take advantage of more favorable terms, payments for principal and interest will exceed US$18 billion in 1986. France will be obliged to borrow to cover its debt service because, while the current account is predicted to be exactly in balance at that time, other capital inflows will be insufficient to cover obligations. The debt service ratio, still comparatively modest at ±9.5% this year, will be rising toward ±13.5% by the end of the forecast period under current projections. The 1984 debt service fluctuated by ±Ffr2.2 billion for every ±1.0% change in LIBOR and by ±Ffr430 million for every ±1.0% change in the US$:Ffr rate. A European Monetary System (EMS) realignment will be postponed until early 1986, when a weakening dollar permits the Dutch guilder and German mark to rise as much as their low inflation and strong trade performances warrant. The budget deficit in 1985 will again exceed its target but should remain a relatively low percentage of GDP (3.8%).

Assessment of Qualitative Factors

Sophisticated financial technocrats will be subject to some political interference during the 1986–88 political transition period, but the commitment to sound management is shared by all major parties. France continues to receive excellent terms; spreads of 0.375% to 0.50% over LIBOR are usual. Floating rate notes at 0.125% over six-month LIBOR have been well received by the markets.

Sociopolitical and Business Forecast

The country will have a Socialist president (until 1988) and a right-of-center Assemblée Nationale (beginning in June 1986). The Gaullist RPR under Jacques Chirac is likely to be the dominant partner in the subsequent coalition with the centrist UDF. Chirac, or the unaffiliated Raymond Barre (prime minister under Giscard d'Estaing) are the most likely presidential winners in 1988. However, because of the present opposition's divisions, coupled with a strong showing for the extreme right and increased fractionalization due to changes in the electoral system, a small probability exists that the Socialists will form a coalition government in 1986. The business environment will continue to improve in the short term. Real GDP will rise 2% in 1985, and momentum will continue into the first half of 1986. Inflation will fall to 5%. Fiscal and social charges on industry will ease this year. Government spending will be up in the preelectoral 1986 budget.

India—2

The political system has survived the trauma of Prime Minister Indira Gandhi's assassination, but there are structural weaknesses that will contribute to future instability: (1) the institutional atrophy of the Congress (I) party, which Mrs. Gandhi converted into an instrument of personalist rule; (2) tensions between central and state governments; (3) bitter ethnic, religious, and class divisions, as seen in Punjab, Assam, and almost every state; (4) border conflicts, primarily with Pakistan, but also with the PRC; and (5) financial imbalances that limit capacity to provide social programs. Rajiv Gandhi, confirmed as prime minister after the December 1984 landslide election, will not be able to make significant progress in correcting these situations and restoring credibility to government. The society is highly politicized, and this deeply affects any form of foreign participation in the economy. Other negative factors in the economic picture include a poorly developed infrastructure, inadequate power supplies, and a low work ethnic. Liquidity will be adversely affected by a slowdown in expatriate remittances and rising debt repayment obligations in 1986–87.

Assessment of Quantitative Factors

India's debt problems are not as serious as those of many Third World countries. If Rajiv Gandhi makes progress in reducing bureaucratic obstacles for business, some gains in manufacturing for export will be made. The present economy is dependent upon uncertain agricultural conditions; 1983–84 witnessed a record grain harvest of 153 million tons; but a drought cycle will cause poor harvests in the late 1980s, and foreign exchange reserves will be required to purchase food overseas. Punjab State, India's most productive agricultural area, is under military rule, and its future is uncertain. In 1984 a trade deficit of US$5,750 million (US$4,266 million in 1983) was registered. Bartering is being used to conserve foreign exchange (equivalent to 3.3 months of imports in mid-1984). The current account deficit rose last year to ±US$3.8 million because of a reversal of improvements in the trade deficit; also, the surplus on invisibles is being adversely affected by a decline in overseas remittances. Repayments of SDR3.9 billion under the IMF Extended Fund Facility begin in 1985, and by 1988–89 debt service on this will total SDR900 million, exclusive of commercial borrowing.

Assessment of Qualitative Factors

Rajiv Gandhi's technocratic orientation and his desire to encourage foreign investment and privatization of the economy are positive factors. His two most influential advisors have business and managerial backgrounds; however, reforms will be limited by political considerations and an entrenched bureaucracy that is notoriously slow and corrupt. The seventh economic plan (1985–90) will emphasize agricultural development but will involve shortfalls of US$7 billion per year on public sector revenuew. India has depleted most sources for concessionary loans and is turning to commercial banks. In the first half of 1985, US$298 million was borrowed.

Sociopolitical and Business Forecast

Frequent incidents of caste, communal, and ethnic violence in all parts of the country will put great strain on the government. Gandhi will have to postpone completion goals for party reform and meaningful anticorruption campaigns to deal with these threats. Two options are open to him: (1) increasing dependence on the armed forces to maintain order, giving them a political role, and (2) a communal appeal to the caste Hindu majority, deserting Congress (I)'s traditional constituencies, the poor and untouchables. Both pose great dangers for Indian democracy, but his mandate provides a unique opportunity. His leadership style appears to be unusaully pragmatic, and this will increase his credibility. GDP growth of 6.8% in FY1983/84 exceeded projections, and in FY1984/85 the rate will be in the 6% to 7% range. Inflation was 10.1% in 1984.

Indonesia—3

Indonesia is a high-risk borrower for private lenders. The country will require large amounts of foreign exchange from these lenders during 1985–86 and subsequent fiscal years because of declining hydrocarbon revenues, inadequate loans from sources granting concessionary terms, and the needs of 164 million people. It is quite probable that interest will remain current on commercial loans, but principal payments will involve a series of reschedulings. The government will be taking steps to cut convertible currency spending in 1985 after an official crude oil price decrease.

Assessment of Quantitative Factors

The current account deficit was halved in 1984 to US$3.2 billion according to preliminary estimates. This progress was achieved by a first-half surge of oil exports, an overall gain in exports of 5.9%, and a 13.8% reduction in imports. During the year crude oil production averaged 1.386 million b/d, well over the 1.3 million b/d OPEC quota that prevailed for most of the year (now 1.189 million b/d and US$29/bbl, and the oil and gas revenues are 60% of total income (planned to be 64% in 1984–85 but will actually be about 62%). Production will average 1.175 million b/d and the price will average US$26.75/bbl; this will yield 16.6% less hydrocarbon income. Consequently, the official projection of a US$3.4 billion current account deficit is more likely to be US$5.7 billion. The US$3.9 billion in new foreign loans and grants planned for 1985–86 (US$4.3 billion in 1984–85) will actually exceed US$6 billion. After repayments, about US$3.6 billion will be added to public foreign debt if the budget is not modified. Considering the resulting increase to US$40.6 billion in external debt owed by the Jakarta government, it is probable that the Intergovernmental Group on Indonesia (IGGI) will encourage major revisions to improve current account performance to less than US$3 billion.

Assessment of Qualitative Factors

A gap exists between the level of concessionary loans from the IGGI (US$2.45 billion in 1984 including US$100 million in grants) and overall borrowing requirements. This year the soft market for hydrocarbons, a shortfall in convertible currency revenues, and poor planning will cause a repetition of 1983's experience when there were project cutbacks, emergency short-term borrowing, and arrears on trade credits. Commercial lenders will increase spreads, and some will decline to participate in syndications. The 1985–86 budget shows a 22.7% increase in recurring expenses and only a 1.8% increase in development; the objective is to minimize nonrupiah commitments. A VAT system begins with the coming fiscal year,and this will assist tax collections. Subsidies are being reduced (for instance, fuel subsidies are about halved). Other positive steps are being taken to achieve a balance in rupiahs, but Jakarta is not being realistic about foreign exchange generation.

Sociopolitical and Business Forecast

Riots, demonstrations, and published attacks on the Suharto government will take place frequently in the 1980s. Jakarta will not have the revenue to provide social relief, new jobs, and adequate food supplies in densely populated areas. The establishment of Golkar party cadre in each village strengthens grass-roots control and puts an intelligence network in place. President Suharto and the army will retain power and no major changes in personnel and policies will take place as a result of unrest. Real growth was slightly higher in 1984 than in 1983 at 4.6%; this year a decline to 2.5% is probable because of falling crude oil prices. Inflation was 10.7% last year, the same as the average for 1982–84; the rate for 1985 will be about 10%. The closing exchange rate for 1985 is estimated at US$1 = Rp1,175.

Japan—1

The political system and society are among the world's most stable, and Japan's international stature is growing as the government adopts active, though still cautious, diplomatic initiatives in East and Southeast Asia and the Middle East. The economy is becoming internationalized, with the flow of Japanese capital overseas, principally to the United States, the liberalization of financial markets, and new opportunities for foreign firms to participate in joint ventures, particularly in high technology. Profitable operations depend to a large degree on willingness to make long-term commitments, knowledge of the language, culture, and local conditions, and meticulous attention to quality.

Assessment of Quantitative Factors

Trade and current account surpluses have spurred criticism overseas and the danger of protectionism. A top priority is to achieve more balance in the trade account; invisibles are usually in deficit by US$10 billion. High interest rates and equity investment in the United States spurred an outflow of capital in 1984 (when there was a net capital account deficit of US$35 billion), and this trend will continue through 1985. The offsetting surplus on current account was US$36.5 billion in FY1984/85, which could go as high as US$47.5 billion in FY1985/86. Foreign exchange reserves were US$22,283 million at end-1984; this is 49 days' cover on merchandise imports and debits on invisibles. The yen, at US$1 = ¥253.65 on 3 April 1985, will remain depressed against the US$ until late 1985.

Assessment of Qualitative Factors

During FY1984/85 (ended 31 March 1985), GDP grew 4.8%, and BERI S.A. projects a rate of 4% in FY1985/86, reflecting a U.S. economic slowdown. Wages will rise 5% in the coming fiscal year (midpoint between the forecasts of management and labor). Inflation in 1984 was 2.6%, compared to 1.9% in 1983; US$-denominated imports became more expensive. A crucial issue is whether growth can be sustained through domestic demand and increased investment by business or must remain dependent upon export performance. Huge deficits force the government to control spending (payments on national debt equal 23% of government spending, and the debt, nearly all in yen is 150% of GNP); but a high rate of personal savings (25% of household budgets) and low taxes insulate the economy from damage. The prime rate, 5.5% in February 1985, causes low real interest rates, conducive to investment in new fixed assets, R&D, and modernization.

Sociopolitical and Business Forecast

Prime Minister Yasuhiro Nakasone remains popular with the public and enjoys a good reputation overseas, but his position within the ruling Liberal Democratic Party (LDP) is precarious; in October 1984 he faced sharp criticism for his alleged "arrogant" style of leadership not only from opposition LDP factions but also from his own mainstream coalition of LDP factions. Although elected party president for a second two-year term, Nakasone has less freedom to promote needed reforms. There will be a return to a more cautious and low-profile style of leadership, particularly after Nakasone steps down in 1986. Government cautiousness and failure to deal with trade deficits will cause some friction with Japan's Western allies and trading partners. Pressure will grow for Japan to more visibly separate foreign policy from calculations of economic advantage and take a more active (though nonmilitary) role internationally.

Korea (South)—2

External factors will play a key role in greater risk, namely a recession in the United States and other markets beginning in 1986 and their adoption of more restrictive trade measures because of domestic political pressures. Government and private firms are determined to control the debt and improve current account performance. The country's foreign debt will be US$47.4 billion at the end of 1986, significantly below the US$64.5 billion projected for 1986 for 1986 in the 1982–86 economic plan.

Assessment of Quantitative Factors

Exports boomed in 1984. In the first three quarters they grew 31%, 22%, and 11%, respectively, over the same periods in the previous year, the pace of growth reflecting the slowdown in the United States' economy. Imports also grew rapidly, and the trade deficit was US$1.46 billion, 14% less than in 1983 (there is a US$3 billion trade deficit with Japan). Despite expansion of the industrial infrastructure, a sharp increase in exports also means a surge of merchandise imports. In the 1980–84 period, the annual current account deficit was trimmed 72%, but the 1984 figure of US$1.5 billion was US$500 million in excess of government projections. This deficit will grow by small amounts until 1988 when recovery will reverse the trend. An important factor is the decline in construction contracts overseas, providing 3.6% of GDP. Counter to this is the decrease in crude oil prices; the cost of petroleum imports was US$5,815 million in 1984. In 1987 the total could be as low as US$2,500 million on the same volume. Foreign public and private debt was US$43.1 billion at end-1984 (26.4% in short-term debt); the 1984 debt service ratio was 21% on long-term loans but an appalling 55.4% when short-term maturities are included. The net addition in 1985 will be US$2 billion.

Assessment of Qualitative Factors

Efforts to restructure the debt profile will be successful, with the short-term component decreased, though performance on one-year maturities will be a serious problem after 1985. Equity capital flows will be less than current account deficits, causing a continuous need for loans in the 1980s. However, net additions to external debt will be small because of the determination of policy makers to keep the debt under control by curbing government spending and industry borrowing. The FY1985 budget will be 9.7% more than the FY1984 budget, but it will have a surplus in the general account. Interest rate liberalization will proceed through 1985, and foreign banks will be given a chance to develop a greater role in domestic lending.

Sociopolitical and Business Forecast

The transfer of power from Kim Il-sung to his son, Kim Jong-il, in the North (transition to culminate in 1986) will add to tensions between North and South during the 1985–90 forecast period; North Korea's behavior is extremely unpredictable, with quickly alternating periods of thaw and confrontation. The new regime under Kim Jon-il will initiate terrorist tactics to keep the South off balance and to disrupt the major international events scheduled for Seoul in the 1980s. Domestic political liberalization will proceed at a cautious pace, with limited opposition activity permitted. Kim Dae-jung's return will aggravate this process. President Chun's methods are often heavy-handed and alienate large portions of the population. The economy grew 7.5% in 1984, compared to 9.5% in 1983. Because of tight money policies (M_2 grew 7% in 1984; 9–10% is planned for 1985 but 7.5% is more likely), inflation (2.5% in 1984) will be kept in check.

Mexico—4

Rescheduling in early 1985 will save Mexico from default on principal payments, and interest payments will remain current this year. Thereafter, it will be impossible for Mexico to remain prompt due to both declining oil prices and decreasing demand for oil exports. Recovery of the market will not begin until 1988, and the pace will be slow.

Assessment of Quantitative Factors

Accumulation of foreign debt continues. It reached US$95 billion in 1984. The projection of ±US$115 billion by 1990 will not be attained because new credit after 1986 will not be granted by lenders. Foreign reserves grew to over US$8 billion by December 1984 due to rescheduling negotiations. The trade surplus in 1984 equaled the 1983 surplus of US$14 million. After two years of positive current account balances, interest payments will result in a deficit again in 1985. Mexico produced 2.89 million b/d of crude oil last year. The government hopes to increase production 3.5%/year, but this is unrealistic in a contracting market. It is much more likely that substantial decreases will take place. Hydrocarbons constitute 66% of exports. Mexico held oil exports to 1.4 million b/d in November and December 1984, a 6.7% cut from those of the rest of the year, in cooperation with OPEC, at a cost of US$83 million a month; it still maintains OPEC prices, although it is not a member. Mexico is trying to increase the proportion of the more expensive Isthmus light from 42% to 45% of oil exports to raise revenues. Exports will average 1.35 million b/d and yield US$13,425 billion in 1985, down 12.3% from the 1984 level. Present projections result in US$8.6 billion in 1986.

Assessment of Qualitative Factors

Mexico has regained its reputation for honoring financial obligations. On 3 January 1985 Mexico made principal payments of US$250 million to show good faith toward plans to reschedule US$47.8 billion of the public debt due by 1989. The agreement includes the provision for converting some of the dollar loans to other currencies. Mexico will avoid default in 1985 because of these efforts, but falling crude oil prices and lower volume of exports make the situation doubtful for next year. To eliminate part of their foreign debt, some private companies, such as Alfa, which owed US$2.3 billion in 1984, have offered equity shares to their creditors. The government is trying to encourage foreign investment but still limits foreign ownership and other concessions. In January 1985 Mexico rejected an offer by IBM to create a wholly owned subsidiary to build home computers for export if the firm could be excluded from domestic content and other regulations. Known flight capital increased 3% in 1984 from 1983. The government raised the daily devaluation rate of the peso from 13 to 17 centavos on 6 December 1984 to reduce speculation and increase exports; the currency is grossly overvalued relative to inflations, and the country has become an expensive place for tourists. The end-1984 rate of US$1 = P191.88 should have been P236.70 based on the 64.6% inflation.

Nigeria—4

With the oil market becoming steadily weaker, Nigeria faces an alarming financial future. An agreement with the IMF would provide a respite, but the political risk is extreme.

The probable result would be a change in government, which would threaten the present trade debt settlements. If the regime delays meeting the IMF's terms, the possibility of reaching agreement will decrease as the debt service ratio starts to climb beyond 40%.

Assessment of Quantitative Factors

The current account achieved a dramatic surplus of US$530 million in 1984 following huge deficits in 1981–83. After Nigeria defied OPEC and cut its oil price in October 1984, production recovered from July-September levels (1.31 million b/d). During much of last year's fourth quarter, production reached 1.50 b/d, well above the temporarily increased OPEC quota of 1.45 million b/d. Overall production for the year averaged 1.37 million b/d, although the official OPEC quota was 1.3 million b/d until the end of July. Foreign exchange earnings from crude oil in 1984 are estimated at US$13.8 billion, up from US$10.2 billion the year before. These revenues will be significantly lower in 1985 (similar to 1983 revenues) as oil prices move downward. Failure to follow proper maintenance procedures at oil installations may also start to affect output. Domestic consumption of petroleum will prove to be much lower than previously thought (perhaps only 150,000–160,000 b/d) now that smuggling of subsidized oil to neighboring states has been curbed. The ending of Societé Générale de Surveillance's import inspection contract caused a sharp drop in the volume of imports processed during October-November, which will help the 1984 import figures. Delayed imports will be carried forward into 1985, but tight control of imports will be maintained throughout the year. The country has set merchandise imports at US$4.10 billion for 1985, a crushing blow to industry. External public and private debt is presently approaching US$21.5 billion, with debt service estimated at US$3.8 billion for 1984 and a debt service ratio just above 26%. Much higher debt service ratios (35%–50%) are anticipated for 1985–87 because of reduced exports. Foreign exchange reserves amounted to US$974 million last September.

Assessment of Qualitative Factors

Nigeria has balked at IMF conditions for a US$2.6–US3.1 billion three-year credit. A 60% naira devaluation and the reduction of petroleum and other subsidies would cause a price explosion, which the regime fears could produce extreme political instability. Pressure to reach an agreement with the fund will intensify as oil prices decline. Meanwhile progress on the rescheduling of some US$2 billion of insured trade debt has stalled over the insistence of export credit agencies that Nigeria reach an arrangement with the IMF. As an interim measure, the government has agreed to pay some interest on the overdue debt (US$220 million in interest is due early in 1985). Towards the end of 1984 new delays on trade debt and other foreign payments were reported. These delays will mount as the shortage of foreign exchange becomes more severe this year. The 1985 budget is based on oil at US$28/bbl, foreign exchange earnings of US$11.5 billion, and total imports (includes invisibles) of US$9 billion. This optimistic scenario made inadequate provision for debt service or declining oil prices. The actual situation will be very grim.

Sociopolitical and Business Forecast

The northern bias of the regime will add to tension as disaffection grows. Though many political detainees have now been released and some of those sentenced for corruption have had their prison sentences greatly reduced, there is no commitment to national reconciliation. The high level of job losses in the shrinking public and private sectors contributes to the pervasive discontent. Inflation is very high (over 100%). GDP growth will be negative in 1985. The sharp reduction of imports in the last quarter of 1984 is causing fresh disruption to hard-hit local industries, which are suffering drastic shortages of raw materials, equipment, and spare parts.

Philippines—4

The Philippines will remain in de facto default throughout the forecast period. Interest payments will be capitalized, and loans will continue to require restructuring. The government finally renegotiated a small portion of the country's debt, but the IMF's economic stabilization plan contains no measures that will improve the economy's capacity to generate foreign exchange. Austerity requirements will worsen increasingly violent sociopolitical conflict.

Assessment of Quantitative Factors

The IMF's demand for a free float of the peso will help lower the current account deficity to US$1.1 billion in 1985. Import-dependent export industries will be aided by lower local currency costs when converted to other currencies and will not be affected by the increased peso cost of imports. Semiconductor exports average 85% import content. Poor weather has caused long-term damage to major coconut growing areas, and prices for other primary export commodities will remain low. Banks have agreed to provide only US$2.8 billion in new trade credits, while normal commerce requires ±US$4 billion. Therefore, imports will decline another 40%, but merchandise exports will barely match 1984 earnings of US$5.3 billion. The country's creditors have restructured US$5.7 billion of the ±US$30 billion in external debt rather than the US$15 billion that the government sought because many of the 484 commercial lenders no longer believe the regime will carry out required reforms. Already, the government has reneged on promises to raise certain taxes and restrain monetary growth. The result is a growing dependence on foreign aid; however, the 1985 goal of ±US$2.5 billion in concessional loans and grants is patently unrealistic. Foreign exchange reserves at US$484 million in November 1984 barely cover a month's imports of goods and services.

Assessment of Qualitative Factors

Commercial lenders no longer trust Philippine technocrats, who are unable to resist President Ferdinand E. Marcos' efforts to maintain the economy as the private preserve of his family and friends. The new long-term commercial loan of US$925 million is below the US$1.65 billion the government sought and has harsh interest rate terms; while nine years to repay with five years' grace is helpful, interest is at 1.75% over LIBOR. The United States government, which provided US$1 billion in foreign aid in 1984, is seeking to lessen its strategic stake in the Philippines.

Sociopolitical and Business Forecast

The communist insurgency and allied leftist movements will gain increasing strength; the moderate opposition will remain divided. Although General Fabian Ver will be acquited in connection with the 1982 assassination of Benigno S. Aquino, Jr., he will be forced to resign. Marcos loyalists will retain control of the armed forces, causing increased discontent among professionally oriented officers. Fidel Ramos will be the person who forces Marcos out of office. Ensuing governments will not be able to prevent anarchy. Austerity policies, after a decade of declining living standards and rising poverty, will fuel violent unrest in both urban and rural areas. GNP will decline by another ±5% in 1985 and will not register growth until 1989–90. High import costs will keep inflation at 50% in 1985 (49.2% in 1984), and interest rates will remain at 40% (21.4% nominal prime) because of IMF monetary policy requirements. The communist movement will become stronger but will be unable to seize power. The socioeconomic situation will have deteriorated too far for any coalition to restore order. The military will again intervene near the end of the decade.

Saudi Arabia—1

A worldwide recession with lower oil prices in 1986–87 and regional political instability contribute to a decline in financial conditions. In addition, the future of the economy depends in large part upon the success of hydrocarbon processing and petrochemicals, which are entering already highly competitive world markets characterized by substantial overcapacity.

Assessment of Quantitative Factors

Saudi Arabia has taken unrealistic positions in attempting to hold OPEC together and is jeopardizing its secure financial position by being the buffer on volume. Internally, cutbacks have occurred. Government spending has decreased to 45% of GDP and was US$64 billion in FY1983/84, the lowest level in four years. Expenditures are targeted for US$73.9 billion in FY1984/85, a 16% increase, based on unrealistic expectations of increasing revenues. Revenues are officially projected to increase 14% to US$60.8 billion, at least US$4 billion too high with declining oil prices. Given Saudi Arabia's dependence on earnings from capital invested abroad and oil revenues (nearly 100% of exports by value) and the uncertain prospects of its large-scale industrialization (refining capacity in 1985 will reach 1.4 million b/d), the outlook for the forecast period is for negative GDP growth, large current account deficits (±US$14.5 billion in 1984), and continued tightening of public expenditure outside of defense and politically sensitive areas. Defense is the largest expenditure at US$22.4 billion, 30% of the budget. Measures initiated in 1984 will limit imports in 1985 and prevent having to repatriate capital invested abroad. Repatriation could occur in the 1987–88 period, but not 1986.

Assessment of Qualitative Factors

Saudi banks have high liquidity, but creditworthy borrowings are rapidly decreasing in number. The Saudi Arabian Monetary Agency (SAMA) will design instruments to absorb liquidity, such as special new accounts, which will eventually be replaced by securities and government bonds. A competitive banking climate will force banks to improve and streamline their management. Profitability in the future will depend on (1) the mix of interest-free and interest-bearing accounts, (2) the ability to control the quality of loan portfolios, and (3) the curbing of expenses. The overall slowdown of the economy has contributed to smaller growth of assets, deposits, and profits. Loans and other credit were up 27% and 18%, respectively, in 1984, suggesting banks are filling part of the gap caused by the slowdown in government spending and payment delays. These delays (1) affected both local and foreign firms, but the latter were harder hit, and (2) caused cash flow shortages. Many companies are now borrowed to their limits and are undercapitalized, heavily invested in fixed assets with diminishing returns. Therefore, refinancing and company failures are likely. The Saudi syndicated loan market declined (a worldwide trend) an estimated 30% in 1984 to US$2.5 billion; this trend will continue as other capital markets become preferred. Countertrade and "offset" investments will increase.

Sociopolitical and Business Forecast

On a macroeconomic level the Saudi economy has adjusted well to the decline in national income caused by lower oil production and prices. The government has used its huge foreign assets to continue and complete major infrastructure projects while promoting private industrial and agricultural development. Nevertheless, many private fortunes are evaporating. The Fourth Five-Year Plan, starting in 1985, will accelerate the shift from physical infrastructure development to training and manpower development, investment in import substitution industry and agriculture, and operation and maintenance of existing facilities. Consumer purchasing turned cautious despite a variety of subsidies, loans, and welfare payments. The al-Saud family will continue to guide the kingdom with a combination of rewards and repression. The revival of Islamic fundamentalism has encouraged the society to become even more rigid and restrictive. Manpower shortages are compounded by the fact that more than half the population (the women) are discouraged, and sometimes barred, from taking full-time employment. Increased Iraqi attacks on Iranian shipping will encourage retaliatory assaults against Saudi shipping; intermittent terrorist acts and internal sabotage by Iranian-supported extremists are probable.

South Africa—3

Recovery of financial equilibrium after 1985 will stem the decline, but the sociopolitical and financial situation is fragile. The slide in the gold price has continued, causing a sharp drop in the value of the rand. The depreciation of the rand is helping the current account, but South Africa is now on the verge of a foreign exchange crisis, and the government will reimpose exchange control measures. The South African Reserve Bank is establishing a new section to monitor the foreign operations of commercial banks.

Assessment of Quantitative Factors

Economic conditions in 1986–88 will be conducive to a substantial rise in gold prices, but interim effects of a weak rand, extremely high interest rates, and black worker job actions will be structurally damaging. 1985 prices for the metal will be weak. At the beginning of 1985 the price of gold dipped below US$300/ounce for the first time in 25 years. A psychological barrier has been broken, and a further drop is likely. Gold will be reacting to confidence in the U.S. dollar in 1985 and will follow the trend of oil prices in 1986. The near-term prospect of relatively low inflation in Western industrial economies will also dampen demand for gold. The rand reached a record low against the U.S. dollar of 0.4330 (US$1 = R2.3094) on 21 January 1985, 52.9% of the value (0.8185 or US$1 = R1.2217) at the start of January 1984. Because of the major change in the exchange rate, the rand value of gold has risen considerably. The current account deficit was ±US$1325 million. Nongold exports were helped by the sliding devaluation, but overall merchandise exports fell 6.2%; imports increased 3.2% because the discouragement from higher costs in rand was mostly offset by more rand realized from exports. Government spending for 1984–85 rose 9.2% above the original budget estimate and is now estimated at R27.1 billion, up from R24.9 billion. Foreign exchange reserves fell to a precarious US$171 million at end-1984, down sharply from US$484 million the previous month. Official gold reserves were 7.83 million fine troy ounces, but the actual amount is considerably higher.

Assessment of Qualitative Factors

The dramatic decline of the rand has forced continuous reassessment of transactions involving foreign exchange. The Reserve Bank is anxious to monitor the effect of foreign operations on liquidity and solvency. The government, state corporations, and private borrowers are all trapped by the exchange risk of foreign loans. With a prime rate of 25% the South Africans went abroad for captial. Currently, U.S. dollar-denominated principal and interest are 89% more expensive in rand than at the beginning of 1984. The treasury and state corporations have been steady borrowers abroad, usually for moderate amounts. Toward the end of 1984, South African Transport Services borrowed US$30 million at 0.625% over LIBOR for the first three years and 0.75% over LIBOR for the fourth and fifth years.

Sociopolitical and Business Forecast

The new constitution will provoke further violence and a high level of black unrest. The merging of political and labor protest, as seen in the November strike by black workers, is a significant development which alarms both government and business leaders. The pressure on the country about apartheid will be sustained during 1985–88 as the ANC intimidates moderate blacks. Major changes in the internal political structure to give blacks modified participation in the system will take place. South Africans will continue to secure their border through aggressive initiatives in neighboring states. Prime lending rates were reduced to 23% in November 1984 but moved up to 24% in December and returned to 25% early in January 1985. High interest rates will curtail industrial expansion and consumer demand, and 1985 growth will be less than last year's 4.8%, or ±1.5%. Farming will be particularly hard hit. By raising the domestic price of imports, the fall in value of the rand will add to inflation, which will be about 13% in 1985 (11.8% in 1984).

Spain—2

The government's program of "free-market socialism" will achieve some solid economic gains before the 1986 elections. Overall political and economic prospects are brighter than many 1983–84 forecasts, and a crisis scenario has low probability.

Assessment of Quantitative Factors

The combination of a depreciating peseta (-11.6% in 1984 against the U.S. dollar), improved prosperity in North America and Europe (which take 75% of Spanish exports), and depressed domestic demand cut the trade deficit in half to about US$3.5 billion. Higher invisibles receipts helped push the current account into a ±US$1 billion surplus (first since 1979). Another, but lower, surplus is likely in 1985 because the above-mentioned factors will be only moderately less favorable. The effects of admission to the European Community will be negative by 1987. The trade balance will suffer by the "front-end loading" of some tariff cuts, which will leave overly protected Spanish industry at a disadvantage. Actual aid flows will not reach promised levels. Budgetary policy generally restrictive, but the deficit will be higher than projected at over 6% of GDP. Foreign borrowing exceeded US$5.2 billion last year, bringing total outstanding debt to about US$32.8 billion at year-end after repayments.

Assessment of Qualitative Factors

Spain will increase borrowing to meet debt service payments in 1986–88 due to the coincidence of renewed current account problems and limitations on EC aid. The country is trying to diversify its debt and refinance to lower interest payments in the coming crucial period; loans denominated in Japanese, Canadian, and European currencies and in ECUs are being sought. Lender support is reflected in relatively attractive terms; spreads of 0.50% to 0.625% over LIBOR for seven to eight years have been given. A recent ten-year US$500 million state credit will permit the kingdom to issue three- to six-month notes at 13 basis points over LIBOR.

Sociopolitical and Business Forecast

Increased fractionalization of the political spectrum and the mixed consequences of EC membership dampen the political outlook. However, the probability of a second term for Socialist Prime Minister Felipe González (which would have a favorable impact) is rising. The alternative is a weak right-of-center government formed by Alianza Popular; this would involve indecision and a backsliding trend of nationalism. In the elections due by October 1986, the prime minister will benefit from demonstrable economic progress (which helps defuse the backlash over his austerity programs) and initial enthusiasm over EC accession (which reduces the bitterness over his "sellout" on NATO). The business environment in 1985 will be characterized by respectable growth (±2.5% again this year), continued subinflationary wage increases achieved by the tripartite economic and social pact, and declining inflation (9.5% after 11.2% in 1984). Unemployment, at 21% will prompt new job-creation incentives, but regard for the Spanish blue-collar worker by investors is not high, and new projects tend to emphasize labor-saving equipment; the trend has been to upgrade skill levels among employees and reduce the probability of confrontation with management.

Taiwan (ROC)—1

Continued economic recovery in 1984 in the United States, the market for almost half of Taiwan's exports, spurred overall export growth of 30% over the previous year, although there was a slowdown in the last two quarters of 1984. Adopting policies of budgetary conservatism, the government has restrained inflation (deficits were less than 2% of GNP in FY1983/84 and are expected to be about 1.2% of GNP in FY1984/85). Foreign debt obligations pose no obstacle to future economic growth, as Taiwan converts to high technology and more value-added export products. However, a recession in the United States and other markets beginning in 1986 will cause political interests in these countries to agitate for trade restrictions that would be damaging to an economy 55% dependent on exports.

Assessment of Quantitative Factors

Taiwan had a balance of trade surplus of US$7.4 billion in 1984, an increase of 52.2% over that of the previous year; the surplus with the United States was a massive US$9.8 billion. The country has registered large surpluses in current account during 1982–84; the 1984 figure, US$6.4 billion, is almost triple the US$2.2 billion in 1982. Performance in 1985 will be good; the recession will begin to have an impact on international balances only in early 1986. During the remainder of the forecast period the decline in oil prices will assist the trade balance as export markets contract. During 1984 the government reduced total foreign debt from US$9.2 billion to less than US$8 billion and slowed the inflow of further loan funds because a buildup in foreign exchange might spark inflation. Nevertheless, convertible currency reserves reached US$17.8 billion by end-1984, up 50% from end-1983.

Assessment of Qualitative Factors

Policy makers have attempted through import promotion schemes to rectify trade imbalances, particularly with the United States, but with limited success. Modernization of financial institutions will remain a high priority during the 1980s. Offshore banking was established in May 1984 as a way of attracting capital from Hong Kong and improving the quality of local banking; research in Hong Kong indicates a reluctance to commit large sums to Taiwan. Terms for foreign banks operating in the domestic economy are being liberalized. Fiscal conservatism and tight controls on borrowing will remain top priorities. Policy makers know that Taiwan's survival depends upon its commercial and financial viability.

Sociopolitical and Business Forecast

Tensions between mainlanders, who are in control of the political system, and native Taiwanese, 85% of the population, are being reduced as Taiwanese gain responsible positions in the Kuomintang (they compose 70% of the total membership) and enjoy economic advantages. Political liberalization will continue, and succession after President Chiang Ching-kuo, who is 75, will be peaceful. During the next five years, informal ties with the People's Republic of China will grow, although the final status of Taiwan will remain unresolved until a new generation of leaders is firmly in place and the PRC's actual performance in Hong Kong is reassuring or otherwise. A relatively equal distribution of the country's wealth and investments in social infrastructure contribute to stability. In 1984 real growth in GNP was an extraordinary 10.9%, exceeding earlier projections of 8.5%. Inflation (CPI) in 1984 was 1.2% compared to 1.4% in 1983.

United Kingdom—1

The political consensus which buttressed the Conservative Party will erode; the probability of a Labour government in 1988 is limited primarily by that party's internal divisions and the probability that economic recovery will again be occurring. The net foreign exchange benefits of North Sea gas and oil will continue to diminish; lower revenues will also constrain budgetary options. Nevertheless, the country will be managed by superior technocrats and will not have any difficulty meeting its modest debt service requirements.

Assessment of Quantitative Factors

Current account performance will fluctuate over the forecast period. It is unlikely that the trade account will regain the surplus achieved in 1980–82. With foreign demand strong in 1984–85, the outcome is still a deficit of ±US$5 billion because (1) petroleum exports are earning less foreign exchange, (2) British-manufactured products lack competitiveness, and (3) import penetration is rising (although the severe fall in the pound sterling will stem this source of the problem). The decline in invisibles surplus has been arrested, in part because of the improved performance of financial services but above all due to the steady stream of income from overseas assets. The current account deficit will, therefore, drop to about US$300 million this year (US$1 billion in 1984) but widen as oil prices drop and international trade slows after this year. The Public Sector Borrowing Requirement (PSBR) will be overshot for the third year in a row, but the general trend is downward. The PSBR is now a modest 2.5% of GDP. Declining oil prices are offset by the strong dollar, which boosts oil revenues in pound sterling.

Assessment of Qualitative Factors

The United Kingdom has exceptionally strong intangible factors affecting its repayment of international obligations. The "city" in London will offer superior financial services and expertise. Economic and financial management under any government will be sophisticated. There is likely to be some outflow of capital prior to the 1988 elections, but a crisis scenario has very low probability. Refinancing activity has permitted established borrowers to obtain 0.25% over LIBOR; other rates for private borrowers and some local governments range from 0.50% to 0.625% for seven to eight years.

Sociopolitical and Business Forecast

Unemployment (12.9%) has been a nonissue while recovery expanded, but the prime minister will begin to distance herself from the unpopular aspects of Thatcherism and accept Keynesian stimulus and job-creation programs in her last two budgets in an attempt to outflank the opposition. Economic recovery will be beginning as the campaign begins. The election will, therefore, depend on the Labour Party's success in isolating its dynamic left wing and in consolidating a youthful leadership under Neil Kinnock, whose performance has been disappointing. The business environment in 1985 will reflect stronger growth because of the coal strike ending; real GDP will rise about 3% this year (2.5% in 1984, down one percentage point because of the strike). Despite real wage gains of 5.5% in the past three years, total labor costs remain substantially below the norm for industrialized countries. With profits up, investment will rise 7%, although the increase in the prime rate to 14% will have a dampening affect.

Venezuela—4

Improvements in Venezuela's financial future following the September 1984 debt rescheduling have been overshadowed by the deterioration in petroleum markets. The new agreement calls for principal repayments of US$5.5 billion in 1989 and an additional US$14.5 billion by 1997, but this agreement will prove inadequate considering Venezuela's dependence on oil for export earnings and the continuing fall in oil prices and export volume. The economic situation for 1985 is not encouraging, and political pressures will make austerity measures increasingly difficult to implement.

Assessment of Quantitative Factors

Venezuela's absolute dependence on oil exports has undermined its financial viability well beyond end-decade. A drop in the average price to US$26/bbl in 1985 and US$20.00/bbl in 1986 will be damaging. Oil output in 1985 will average 1.55 million b/d; foreign exchange earnings from oil will be US$12.8 billion. Last year output averaged 1.77 million b/d (OPEC quota of 1.675 million b/d until it was cut to 1.555 million b/d late in the year); exports yielded US$14.9 billion in earnings. Volume of exports rose 2.2% in 1984. Under such conditions, Venezuela will not be able to keep current on its interest payments, even under the favorable terms agreed to in the September 1984 rescheduling. Principal will not begin to be recovered in this decade. Attempts to diversify exports into nonpetroleum areas have not proved and will not prove successful because of high investment costs, a severe shortage of available capital, and weak investor confidence. An estimated US$20 billion is held overseas by Venezuelans, and repatriation to Venezuela is unlikely any time in the near future. Exchange controls have also been barriers to domestic manufacturing expansion. Imports have not recovered to pre-1983 levels but approached US$10 billion in 1984; they will show only modest gains in 1985. Therefore, the year-end trade surplus will be approximately US$3.5 billion, contributing to a substantial current account deficit (assuming interest payments are prompt).

Assessment of Qualitative Factors

The rescheduling of US$20.75 billion of foreign debt with the 13-bank advisory committee (to be formally signed in the second quarter of 1985) indicates a new determination on the part of the Lusinchi government to confront the debt problem rather than to ignore it, as has been the approach in the past. Approximately 75% of the US$36 billion debt is public, and interest payments should continue on schedule. Of greater concern is the private debt, which has fallen over US$1 billion in arrears. Much of this arrearage can be attributed to the inefficiency of Recardi, the agency that oversees the debt and decides who gets favorable exchange rates. Delays are lengthy, and many companies have simply ceased making repayments. A "consulting" industry has sprung up to expedite claims, and corruption is widespread. Lusinchi's attempts to halt corruption and to impose austerity measures similar to those in Mexico and Brazil indicate a current improvement in attitude, but it is unlikely that these measures will significantly change current trends.

Sociopolitical and Business Forecast

The economy will continue to be weak in 1985, although improved over last year. GDP will break even in real terms because of the decreased oil industry activity. Agricultural and industrial output will repeat the 3% increase registered in 1984, but other industries such as construction will be down. Unemployment will continue to be high, with the official percentage at year-end likely to be 15% (actual rate will be closer to 20%). These figures, combined with the decline of per capita GDP and the continuation of high inflation rates, will produce growing political problems for the Lusinchi administration. Labor unions will become more active. Operating conditions will continue to deteriorate as the credit squeeze tightens and nationalistic laws are implemented. Currently, commercial payments, dividends, and royalties held up by Recardi are estimated at US$2 billion.

4

The Role of Crude Oil Prices

The OPEC price hikes in October 1973 from US$3.39/barrel [OPEC posted prices weighted by average production unless otherwise indicated] to US$11.28/barrel and subsequent increases culminating in the October 1981 price accord at US$34.55/barrel are exogenous events in business cycle theory. The probability for a worldwide financial crisis rose with each OPEC increase. The following four paragraphs introduce the main sections of this chapter and summarize the impact on advanced and developing economies.

First, despite soft petroleum markets in 1982–85 and the official retreat from the pricing peak to the US$28.20/barrel announced in February 1985, paying more than US$18/barrel is a form of entrapment for economies with limited energy resources. Billion and billions in foreign exchange were spent during the past three decades on industrialization in the form of energy-consuming plants producing electricity, steel, heavy machinery, and other traditional products. These activities provide jobs. Improved living standards, and fundamental necessities. Changes needed to escape the oil import trap require a high level of human resources and capital investment. The advanced countries are progressing with painful economic restructuring, but most developing nations do not have adequate resources to escape from heavy dependence on expensive crude oil.

The second aspect of the OPEC price decisions surfaced in the late 1970s. It has become necessary to use large portions of foreign loans to pay for "consumables" (oil, food, interest, and principal payments) instead of spending the funds on plant and equipment, which increase export capacity, productivity, and output per capita. Infrastructure additions needed to earn convertible currency, such as seaport modernization and an expanded transportation system, are being postponed or curtailed. Even maintenance is at low levels. The investment needed to maintain economic growth, provide jobs, and develop natural resources is not taking place in the 1980s to the degree that occurred in the 1970s. As a consequence, most net oil importing economies are actually contracting relative to financial and social requirements.

The third factor discussed in Chapter 4 involves trade between countries. Volume greatly increased during the 1970s, but it has contracted seriously in this decade. One of the strongest motivations in the 1970s was the need to generate foreign exchange to pay for imported oil. A few strong, competently managed economies have consistently achieved current account surpluses despite energy imports. However, the vast majority of oil importing countries are running immense current account deficits year after year. If they correct their international balances, they cripple their internal economy.

This is the situation in which recycling petrodollars becomes a factor in the potential financial crisis. Huge volumes of U.S. dollars were flowing into banks in industrialized countries seeking interest. To cover the cost of these monies, loans were extended to developing and Eastern Bloc countries under terms that earned attractive profits. But high interest rates, ongoing current account deficits, and internal fiscal problems made debt service increasingly difficult. In addition, the drop in crude oil prices greatly reduced the flow of petrodollars and supplies of fresh credits decreased. Some relief occurred during the 1983–85 business recovery. However, as recession began to develop and domestic as well as foreign loans became doubtful assets, some major American banks approached the brink of failure. The contraction in worldwide trade will extend the list of countries in de facto default.

The fourth aspect of crude oil prices in the financial crisis became apparent in 1981. Recession, conservation, and substitution curtailed petroleum purchases. Also, many oil-producing countries, such as Mexico, expanded their production capacity in order to earn hard currency for economic development. Other countries such as Brazil and Chile, invested in crude oil output and lessened the drain on foreign exchange reserves caused by oil imports. Soft markets for petroleum forced net oil exporters to cut back economic programs and to borrow to meet international obligations. As a result, although prices did not decline sufficiently to give adequate relief to importers, several exporters were drawn into the group of financially troubled countries.

ENTRAPMENT

Developing countries have been most affected by the 918% escalation in energy cost (OPEC's production weighted prices, 1973 to 1981). Five examples are shown in Table 4–1. The amounts that could have been invested in economic development rather than buying oil are significant. Equally significant are (1) the upward thrust of amounts lost to development caused by the 1979–80 oil price increases, despite results from conservation programs, and (2) amounts for the 1981–84 period shown in Table 4–2. It appears that a turning point in capacity to cope occurred in 1980.

Some progress in reducing the impact of oil purchases on capital formation is evident in 1981–84, the average amount lost from development is estimated to be about double the percentages in the 1974–78 period. The worldwide situation for countries is similar to a company incurring a 918% increase in the cost of a critical component for a product. It is crushing if the cost cannot be passed on to the customer through a price increase or if productivity and technological advances cannot offset a substantial portion of the added cost. The majority of the countries have not been able to adjust, even though such adjustment is feasible.

For example, Japanese companies have retained price competitiveness through industriousness, petroleum product substitution, and design ingenuity. Pragmatic compromise and hard work permitted them to control unit costs and improve quality. Gross capital formation has remained high and the shift away from oil entrapment has been more rapid than in other countries, despite Japan's almost total dependency on these imports. This is illustrated in Table 4–3.

Generally, advanced countries are attempting to free themselves from entrapment by (1) encouraging private enterprise to develop high technology- low energy-consuming products that have competitive advantages in international markets, (2) sourcing from other countries all

TABLE 4-1. Percentage of Actual Gross Capital Formation Lost from Funds Diverted to Oil Purchases* (US$ millions)

	1973	1974	1975	1976	1977	1978	1979	1980	Eight Years
Brazil									
Petroleum Imports	986	3,233	3,300	4,083	4,201	4,617	6,918	10,355	37,675
Petroleum Imports No Price Change*	986	990	1,007	1,227	1,247	1,440	1,798	1,806	10,501
Amount Lost from Development	-0-	2,243	2.293	2,856	2,954	3,177	5,102	8,549	27,174
% of Actual Gross Capital Formation		8.7	7.3	8.2	8.1	7.5	11.0	16.4	
Korea (ROK									
Petroleum Imports	277	966	1,271	1,607	1,934	2,190	3,104	5,640	16,989
Petroleum Imports No Price Change*	277	296	388	483	574	683	807	984	4,492
Amount Lost from Development	-0-	670	883	1,124	1,360	1,507	2,297	4,656	12,497
% of Actual Gross Capital Formation		14.3	16.8	17.3	14.9	10.4	11.8	25.5	
India									
Petroleum Imports	308	1,165	1,152	1,060	1,753	2,024	3,067	6,022	16,551
Petroleum Imports No Price Change*	308	357	351	319	520	631	797	1,050	4,333
Amount Lost from Development	-0-	808	801	741	1,233	1,393	2,270	4,972	12,218
% of Actual Gross Capital Formation		6.1	5.1	4.5	6.2	5.7	8.6	16.3	

Spain									
Petroleum Imports	1,062	3,443	3,559	4,481	4,468	4,651	6,597	11,344	39,914
Petroleum Imports No Price Change*	1,062	1,055	1,085	1,347	1,326	1,450	1,715	1,978	11,018
Amount Lost from Development	-0-	2,388	2,774	3,143	3,142	3,201	4,882	9,366	28,896
% of Actual Gross Capital Formation		10.9	11.4	14.5	12.6	11.2	13.0	23.4	
Turkey									
Petroleum Imports	222	763	810	1,126	1,470	1,297	1,732	3,579	10,999
Petroleum Imports No Price Change*	222	234	247	338	436	404	450	624	2,955
Amount Lost from Development	-0-	529	563	788	1,034	893	1,282	2,955	8,044
% of Actual Gross Capital Formation		9.7	8.0	8.3	9.6	8.4	9.9	32.1	

*The 1973 Ras Tanura price of US$2.70 was adjusted for the rate of inflation rate in the United States and the resulting prices were: 1974, US2.99; 1975, US$3.27; 1976, US$3.46; 1977, US$3.68; 1978, US$3.96; 1979, US$4.41; and 1980, US$5.00. The methodology involves a ratio of the adjusted price and the actual annual average price. The resulting decimal is applied to actual oil purchases by a country to derive what they would have paid for oil without the series of price increases. The difference is the amount lost to development.

TABLE 4-2. Percentage of Gross Capital Formation Lost from Funds Diverted to Oil Purchases*

	1981	1982	1983E	1984E
Brazil				
Petroleum Imports	11,723	10,878	8,888	8,250
Petroleum Imports No Price Change*	1,991	1,905	1,830	2,015
Amount Lost from Development	9,732	8,973	7,058	6,235
% of Gross Capital Formation	17.6	17.1	11.3	10.1
Korea				
Petroleum Imports	6,376	6,093	5,577	5,625
Petroleum Imports No Price Change*	1,083	1,067	1,110	1,240
Amount Lost from Development	5,293	5,026	4,467	4,385
% of Gross Capital Formation	29.8	26.1	18.7	18.1
India				
Petroleum Imports	5,942	5,110	3,981	3,250
Petroleum Imports No Price Change*	1,009	895	785	725
Amount Lost from Development	4,933	4,215	3,196	2,525
% of Gross Capital Formation	14.7	12.6	8.3	7.1

Spain				
Petroleum Imports	9,893	10,096	9,025	8,750
Petroleum Imports No Price Change*	1,680	1,768	1,915	2,080
Amount Lost from Development	8,213	8,328	7,110	6,670
% of Gross Capital Formation	22.1	24.2	23.7	22.0
Turkey				
Petroleum Imports	3,871	3,738	3,653	3,300
Petroleum Imports No Price Change*	657	654	670	735
Amount Lost from Development	3,214	3,084	2,983	2,565
% of Gross Capital Formation	34.4	33.6	24.5	20.5

*Please refer to the footnote of Table 4-1. The inflation adjusted price of oil per barrel (Ras Tanura basis) are: 1981, US$5.52; 1982, US$5.86; 1983, US$6.06; and 1984, US$6.40.

but strategic minimums of products with processes that require important use of energy, (3) inducing conservation and transition to a different industrial profile by selectively raising the cost of petroleum products, (4) emphasizing development and sale of problem-solving services, patents, and systems to earn foreign exchange, and (5) sponsoring research and development that lead to new energy sources.

During the coming years Germany, Japan, Switzerland, and a few others will be transformed into "headquarters countries" with concentrations of highly trained people, a sophisticated infrastructure, technology-based operations, a low number of plants in traditional industries, and sharply reduced requirements for oil. This transformation will involve the application of high quality human resources.

TABLE 4-3. Percentage of Gross Capital Formation Lost from Funds Diverted to Oil Purchases

	1974-76	1977-79	1980-81
Japan	9.2	7.8	13.9
Five Country Average	10.1	9.9	23.2

Most of the 65 countries included in the research do not have a realistic chance of becoming "headquarters countries." For example, Belgium has the potential and has shown some pragmatism during 1982–85 in correcting the excesses that developed in the 1970s; however, bickering between ethnic/language groups and a high degree of political fragmentation illustrates specific limitations in human resources. Australia's labor force does not have the work ethnic needed for a "headquarters country." Brazil, Korea, and Spain are good examples of entrapment, although Korea and Spain have made superior progress toward escaping after reachieving political stability. The extensive investment in heavy energy consuming industry by developing countries in recent decades condemns them to: (1) current account deficits, (2) foreign borrowing, and (3) deep cutbacks in imports, investment, and economic growth to limit unmanageable expansion of international obligations. It will take strong gifted leaders to optimize resources and reduce the impact of austerity on the population. Particularly important in this effort is the combined human resources in a country. Table 4–4 shows an assessment of these resources for selected countries.

TABLE 4-4. Ratings for an Assessment of Human Resources* (100 = optimal human resources)

	Highest Twelve			Selected Others	
	Present	+5 Years		Present	+5 Years
Switzerland	93.8	94.0	Argentina	40.7	40.5
United States	36.2	85.0	Australia	60.8	62.5
Japan	84.3	85.0	Brazil	47.6	49.0
Germany	83.7	82.5	France	59.2	58.0
Singapore	79.0	82.0	India	31.3	31.5
Sweden	78.6	77.5	Ivory Coast	33.4	30.0
Netherlands	74.2	73.0	Kenya	32.5	31.0
Belgium	68.9	67.0	Korea (ROK)	58.8	60.0
Norway	66.8	67.0	Malaysia	46.7	46.0
Taiwan (ROC)	65.1	67.0	Mexico	39.3	37.5
Canada	63.7	63.0	South Africa	59.4	48.0
Denmark	63.5	63.0	Spain	51.0	52.0

*Refer to Appendix A for methodology.

The ratings for *Assessment of Human Resources* require interpretation.

1. Countries with an index of less than 60.0 have a low probability of transforming their economies to a modern industrial profile after a foreign debt solution is implemented. The likelihood of long-term entrapment is high. This means that most of the net oil importers are in fundamental trouble, regardless of the fall in crude oil prices foreseen in the last section of this chapter and solutions to the financial crisis suggested in Part II. Economic development will not provide adequate jobs nor the export capacity to earn hard currency and service debt. When high population growth rates are combined with low human resources ratings and the country does not have high volume commodity exports, an explosive sociopolitical situation is evolving.

2. Countries with heterogeneous populations require special analysis. The United States, for example, has the largest economy in the world. It received a high rating. Yet, the skills of a large portion of the people are only

suitable in traditional industries, and as much as 15% of the workforce (including illegal aliens) is unemployable in a "headquarters country." India, noted for two separate economies (one modern with a relatively advanced workforce and a vast ancient society), is a reverse example; the country's talented human resources are overwhelmed in the ratings by huge numbers existing outside the modern economy. Between the extremes are countries, such as France, with pockets of superior people who will outperform averages.

3. Authoritarian governments will tend to optimize the use of available human and physical resources, although the beneficiaries are often an elite group at the top of society. When nepotism and repression are also present in the country, talented people tend to leave for more attractive environments. Singapore is an example of success in escaping entrapment through full use of human resources. Strategically located but with no natural resources, Lee Kuan Yew has created a stable environment for banking, processing (third largest refinery complex), technology-based industry, and a variety of services. On the other hand, alternating Argentine civilian and military governments have exhibited extraordinary incompetence. While the country is potentially self-sufficient in energy and has proven agricultural export capacity, thereby escaping entrapment, Argentina will flounder below its potential due to lack of human resources.

4. Expatriate workers are not included in the ratings. Saudi Arabia has made progress in training its own people, but it still augments the labor force by importing people to work at all levels. South Africa contracts for basic labor from Mozambique and needs skilled personnel. Both are examples of affluent countries that are able to fill the voids in their human resources because they have natural resources and entrapment is not a factor. However, oil importing countries in Africa using expatriate administrators to run ministries and agencies will be trapped. The leadership will be influenced by unemployment, nationalism, and the drain on reserves caused by expatriate remittances and will decrease the number of work permits.

Summarizing for entrapment, the developing countries making the most progress in recent years as measured by the standard industrialization model are now unable to supply energy to these facilities without accumulating foreign debt. Interest obligations on past debt are rising at nearly the same pace as the fall in petroleum prices. The capital committed to projects in heavy traditional industry does not earn adequate convertible currency to meet the foreign obligations incurred, nor do these operations substitute for a sufficient volume of imports to justify the investments. Internal factors, including the saving of existing jobs, national pride, and avoiding exposure of miscalculation by leaders, result in the decision to continue operations.

Steps required to change the composition of the economies depend on a broadly high level of human resources. The capacities to compromise, endure, and behave with minimal corruption, greed, and conflict of interest is basic. Even in advanced countries, the people commonly lose confidence in leaders who attempt to restructure their economies because years of high unemployment and personal insecurity are involved before the basis for long-term recovery is visible to the work force and their families.

BORROWING FOR CONSUMABLES

A measure was conceived by the author to indicate whether a country is applying too much of its foreign exchange earnings to consumables and inadequate amounts to capital goods. The *Saturation Measure* consists of petroleum imports plus debt service (interest and principal) as a percentage of total foreign exchange received from merchandise exports, credit for services, and net unrequited transfers in a year. Theoretically, a country should not be loaned additional funds when saturation occurs (defined as 60% and over). The results for 14 countries are given in Table 4–5.

The turning point for developing countries becomes clear in the Saturation Measure as well as the Capital Lost from Economic Development statistics. A few of the more advanced developing countries have the advantage of having currencies that are accepted in international transactions, although the U.S. dollar is required for petroleum and many other commodities and products. Problems created by the excessive borrowing of these governments within their own borders were discussed in Chapter 1.

Developing countries, however, rarely have fully convertible currencies. When saturation exists, or when a definitive trend toward saturation develops, it can be corrected only through restructuring of the economy. This implies lower living standards and the potential sociopolitical instability covered in Chapter 5. For example, in 1977 coffee exports from Brazil earned a record US$2,299 million and paid for 41% of interest and principal on total foreign

TABLE 4-5. Saturation Measure (in percentage: 60% to 100% = Saturation)

	1973	1974	1975	1976	1977	1978	1979	1980	1981	1982	1983
Advanced Countries											
Belgium	5.3	11.1	9.7	10.2	9.3	8.4	11.1	12.7	14.8	15.7	15.9
France	7.7	16.1	14.2	15.8	14.1	11.4	12.8	17.0	16.5	16.7	18.6
Germany	6.9	11.6	10.6	11.3	10.4	9.2	12.7	10.3	9.9	8.3	8.1
Japan	15.1	31.9	30.8	28.9	27.0	22.5	30.1	36.6	32.4	28.8	25.0
South Africa	13.8	14.1	15.3	15.5	14.8	14.6	20.9	14.2	21.1	25.2	27.5
Taiwan (ROC)	5.4	13.6	13.8	14.6	16.0	15.2	20.2	25.9	29.0	21.0	20.7
United States	6.9	17.8	17.0	19.9	23.5	22.1	20.5	22.6	22.3	22.7	21.7
Developing Countries											
Brazil	45.1	66.1	75.4	74.5	72.9	88.4	100.3	100.1	107.4	117.7	117.0
India	26.7	40.4	30.5	23.6	28.0	26.9	33.8	45.4	50.5	32.1	30.2
Kenya	10.4	11.9	11.8	11.8	7.0	10.2	14.9	30.3	33.9	40.5	50.6
Korea (ROK)	20.8	24.0	32.5	26.4	24.2	23.4	28.9	37.8	41.6	38.8	37.2
Philippines	14.2	19.8	32.0	35.4	32.8	42.4	39.7	34.6	41.3	46.5	47.8
Spain	12.1	26.9	27.7	31.9	29.0	29.5	30.3	40.6	39.8	41.0	43.5
Turkey	10.4	27.5	31.2	36.3	49.7	41.7	54.4	85.5	66.9	63.8	64.9
Average for Advanced Countries	8.7	16.6	15.9	16.6	16.4	14.8	18.3	19.9	20.9	19.8	19.6
Average for Developing Countries	20.0	30.9	34.4	34.3	34.8	37.5	43.2	53.5	54.5	54.3	55.9

debt. In 1980 coffee earned a new record of US$2,486 million and paid for only 19% of debt service. In 1983 coffee income was US$2,078 million and this was 12% of payments due (part of debt service was in arrears at year-end).

Track 1

Analysis of the Saturation Measure indicates countries are on three tracks. On Track 1, 60% or more of foreign exchange generation is going to oil purchases and debt service. Severe austerity measures are currently under way, and rescheduling of principal payments is necessary. Rollovers are basic to avoiding default. Future growth is limited by inadequate capital to expand or even maintain present facilities. The sociopolitical framework is potentially unstable as a result of policies required to meet external obligations.

Examples include Argentina, Brazil, Chile, Morocco, Poland, and Zaire. Australia has been borrowing heavily in commercial markets since 1981, and the Saturation Measure reached 69.1% in 1983 (56.5% in 1982). A return to Track 2 occurred in 1984–85; but the developing recession will cause a serious socioeconomic disruption in the country, and capital inflows will not be sufficient to offset chronic current account deficits. Turkey, on the other hand, will benefit from grants and concessionary loans based on its strategic location and from improved export performance under the Ozal government.

Track 2

Between 30% and 59% of foreign exchange earnings is going to oil purchases and debt service. Expansion of the economy and real GDP growth over 3% causes untenable energy consumption, current account deficits, increased foreign debt, and accelerated inflation. Policies to avoid these problems tend to cause unemployment, high interest rates, and low levels of investment. Countries with less than 1.5% net population growth rates, 60 or above in human resource ratings, and stable political systems will tend to decrease their saturation measure in the 1980s.

Countries not meeting these criteria will tend to take steps that increase their Saturation Measure. In these cases, sociopolitical instability also increases, and management of the economy becomes difficult. Those with a tendency to increase include Greece, Kenya, Philippines, Portugal, Spain, and Thailand. Korea (ROK) has achieved extraordinary progress since President Chun Doo-hwan began his single seven-year term in February 1981 and will move closer to Track 3 in future years.

Track 3

Up to 30% of foreign exchange generation is going to oil purchases and debt service. Competitiveness of advanced countries has been selectively hurt by the 918% oil price hike during 1973–81, but some countries have done a remarkable job of management. For example, Saturation Measure results for Taiwan are superior, when it is considered that the country produces only 2,350 barrels/day and pays US$4 billion per year for petroleum imports. On the other hand, unwillingness to trim social benefits, balance budgets, and reduce external borrowing are moving Denmark and Sweden toward Track 2.

The Saturation Measure is not usually compiled for net oil exporters. If only debt service is considered and such other consumables as food and luxury imports are excluded, some of these countries reach Track 1. Ecuador, Nigeria, and Venezuela are examples. Indonesia is on Track 2 due to a high proportion of concessionary loans and relatively low debt service payments. High population growth rates and endemic corruption are common factors that have weakened these economies. Even Malaysia, now on Track 3, is moving toward Track 2 because of external borrowing to relieve socioeconomic pressures, partially caused by a high population growth rate.

In 1986–87, when confidence wanes and countries as well as companies turn defensive, the number of countries moving on to Track 1 will increase dramatically. Export markets will contract for several months even if solutions discussed in Chapters 6 and 7 are applied promptly because a subsequent transition period will occur, during which only scarce fresh credits and barter deals will enable many countries to trade. Revenues from services will fall during this recession. Workers will be returning home instead of remitting convertible currency. However, restructured debt service will be greatly reduced under the proposed solution, and the majority of countries will quickly work their way to the lower levels of Track 2 as the recovery begins with vigor in late 1987. Some will reach Track 3 as the decade ends because the market price for crude oil will have declined to US$21/barrel. Details of this decline are given later in this chapter.

If some combination of proposed solutions are not applied promptly, the several months of transition mentioned above become several years. A short recession becomes a depression. The market price for crude oil returns to US$14/barrel. Prosperity in the remainder of this decade depends on nations' having financial capacity to trade and an orderly transformation of the total loan profiles for all net debtor nations.

FINANCIAL INTERDEPENDENCE

Advanced countries would be affected by a financial crisis as severely as those developing nations fully entrapped by heavy industry that consume large volumes of energy. The "headquarters country" approach, which began to evolve after the 1973 oil price increase, emphasizes sale of sophisticated problem-solving products and services as a means of sustaining growth and generating convertible currency to pay for required imports. International trade would be deeply affected by a sustained economic contraction, and the ability of other nations to pay would be curtailed. Therefore, exports as a percentage of GDP will be an important measure of vulnerability to the crisis. Selected countries are shown in Table 4–6.

TABLE 4-6. Exports as a Percentage of GDP

	Average			Average	
	1976-79	1980-83		1976-79	1980-83
United States	8.5	9.0	Argentina	13.0	9.1
Japan	13.1	15.7	Brazil	7.2	13.2
Australia	16.3	16.0	India	7.0	7.1
France	20.1	22.1	Ireland	51.9	54.0
Germany	27.5	31.6	Kenya	32.6	26.1
Sweden	28.8	32.6	Korea (ROK)	34.5	37.6
South Africa	32.5	29.6	Mexico	9.7	16.0
Switzerland	35.3	35.9	Philippines	18.3	18.8
Belgium	48.3	64.3	Spain	12.1	17.2
Taiwan (ROC)	58.0	53.3	Turkey	5.1	11.8

Japan moved many operations offshore in the 1970s and early 1980s, and additional exports are shown in the statistics of Korea, Taiwan, and other countries. Therefore, sharply decreased trade would hurt the Japanese more than indicated by the percentages. Nevertheless, investment by Japanese companies in the few countries with a relatively low vulnerability is reducing the impact of sustained decline in international trade. Earnings from operations remitted to headquarters will help to pay for much cheaper oil despite loss of export volume. France, Germany, and Switzerland have also greatly increased geographic diversification of operations controlled through ownership and management.

The United States will be the least affected by a decline in international trade. The domestic market is immense, and the percentages in Table 4–6 show a low dependence on foreign markets. Instead, the causes of severe socioeconomic problems in the 1986–90 period are a combination of (1) huge national budget deficits, (2) a tight monetary policy, (3) capital inflows from abroad that created a strong U.S. dollar, and (4) a fragile banking system nearing the breaking point at end-1985. Some movement out of U.S. dollars during the crisis—due to American bank failures and bureaucratic delays in implementing the solutions—would devalue the currency and increase competitiveness, as mentioned in Chapter 1. A core of unemployables would be instigators of demonstrations and riots, but the financial and industrial infrastructure would provide a basis resiliency for economic recovery. It is probable that the United States will lead the world to sustained prosperity in the 1990s after a time for temporary and long-term changes in policy direction.

Each of the 65 countries included in the research requires special analysis for degree of financial interdependence. Spain, for example, depends on international tourism in combination with merchandise exports to generate convertible currency. The volume of visitors will fall after the 1983–85 recovery and spending per tourist will drop. Therefore, debt incurred to pay for deficits in its international balances in the 1970s and the first half of the 1980s would be a severe burden if a financial crisis turns into a depression instead of a short-lived recession.

Mexico's enormous population is increasingly dependent on oil exports (70.3% of total exports in 1983). Even a plateau in revenue has serious socioeconomic impact. Because the market will not bear expansion of volume in relation to falling crude oil prices and rising cash needs, the government will be unable to meet rescheduled loan obligations in 1986. The strategic importance of Mexico, the clear implications of lower crude oil prices, and the obvious shortfall of cash flow in the last half of the decade could be the factors that motivate the American Congress, the Federal Reserve system, and others to consider a global debt solution seriously.

France's experiment in socialism was poorly timed. Nationalizations, reduced private investment, escalating unit costs relative to currency valuation, and a high degree of entrapment laid the foundation for socioeconomic problems and financial imbalances soon after the Socialists took office in 1981. The country has gifted technocrats, and they recognized the scope of dealing with difficulties without compounding their problem by introducing policy changes. This prompted fiscal austerity in 1983–85, and significant improvement also took place in the country's balance of payments. The restructuring of the economy is causing extreme unemployment (defined as over 10%), but leaders advocating strict socialists ideology have much less influence at the end of the five-year term. An optimistic forecast is supported by the near certainty that a right-of-center government will return to power in 1986 and a conservative president will be elected in 1988.

The conclusion for net oil importing countries is that commitment to industrialization that does not emphasize light technology-oriented manufacturing and sale of sophisticated services has resulted in expensive petroleum addiction. Advanced and developing countries are accelerating efforts to increase convertible currency earnings from an industrial cross-section that is less dependent on petroleum, but the financial costs associated with the change are outpacing the returns. Only a few of the 65 countries are close to breakeven or are achieving a surplus on current account. OPEC members began running deficits in 1983. Some examples of performance are given in Table 4–7.

Some Petrodollar Implications

A majority of trade transactions (not just oil payments) are denominated in U.S. dollars, and the world is awash in this currency (refer to Chapter 1). By the late 1980s U.S. monetary integrity will have been challenged, but even with a financial crisis, this cornerstone of the world's monetary system will remain functional. One solution to stabilizing the U.S. dollar during the coming financial troubles is a return to the gold standard.

The final break between the U.S. dollar and gold came in 1971 when central banks were deciding that they would rather have gold than U.S. dollars. The most frequently mentioned system involves the U.S. dollar being freely convertible into gold at a fixed price and a gold "cover" of

TABLE 4-7. Current Account Performance

	1983 Surplus (US$ millions)		1983 Deficit (US$ millions)
Germany	4,002	Argentina	2,436
Japan	20,804	Australia	5,445
Mexico	5,208	Belgium	762
Netherlands	3,681	Brazil	6,837
Norway	2,204	France	4,904
South Africa	320	India	2,452
Switzerland	3,526	Kenya	177
Taiwan (ROC)	4,470	Korea (ROK)	1,607
United Kingdom	3,419	Malaysia	2,847
		Nigeria	4,738
		Philippines	2,758
		Saudi Arabia	18,433
		Spain	2,480
		Sweden	938
		Turkey	1,747
		United States	41,580

50%. Currency in the United States amounts to about US$550 billion at end-1984. Holdings outside the country, as mentioned, equal about US$750 billion. Therefore, about US$1,300 billion could be converted. The United States at end-1984 had 263 million troy ounces of gold. Using the 50% cover, the price of gold would have to be US$2,470 per ounce.

The possibility of the United States' assuming a gold standard must be considered remote. The U.S. dollar would stabilize at early 1985 levels, which were extremely high relative to record budget and current account deficits. Sustaining the U.S. dollar at these exchange rates would disrupt trade and cause havoc in international financial markets. Commodities denominated in U.S. dollars, such as petroleum, would become extremely expensive in local currency cost for a long period of time despite soft market conditions. External debt service would take on crushing dimensions. American products would be extraordinarily expensive and competitors of U.S. companies would have a substantial price advantage. The U.S. government will not make this unilateral decision in the face of domestic and international pressures.

The conclusion is that the post-World War II monetary system based on a strong U.S. dollar will be modified to reflect (1) a basic devaluation of the U.S. dollar from peaks achieved during 1985 and (2) banking regulations and reserve requirements to prevent another accumulation of unmanageable debt. When recovery begins in 1988 or 1989, the U.S. dollar will continue to be the medium for international trade, and realistic exchange rates will facilitate competition.

THE IMPACT OF EXCESS CRUDE OIL PRODUCTION CAPACITY

In mid-1981 it became apparent that crude oil production capacity significantly exceeded demand. Prices and output dropped as net oil importers stepped up conservation measures, consumed less in the developing recession, and substituted other forms of energy. Critically important, many net oil importing nations such as Brazil and Ivory Coast increased domestic crude oil output and purchased less. Mexico became a major factor, production increasing from 1.082 million barrels/day (b/d) in 1976 to 2.693 million b/d in 1983. In addition, North Sea output reached 2.925 million b/d in 1983.

The October 1981 price accord by OPEC was intended to stabilize the situation by consolidating member prices around a higher Saudi Arabian market price (US$34/barrel instead of US$32/barrel) and reducing output to 19 million b/d, mostly by Saudi Arabia cutting production to 8 million b/d. The price of crude oil continued to fall in the spot market, and several OPEC members broke the agreement and offered substantial discounts. In March 1982 an emergency OPEC meeting resulted in a production cut to 17.5 million b/d. This move made no significant progress in reducing inventories, and by March 1983 market conditions had deteriorated. A US$5/barrel price cut was made and the market became US$29/barrel. Oversupply depressed spot market prices in 1984; in October production quotas were reduced to a total of 16.5 million b/d, but OPEC had difficulty reaching agreement on a price reduction. Finally, the organization lowered most crude oil by US$1/bbl in early 1985. Table 4–8 shows crude oil supply.

The capacity utilization trend plateaued in 1984–85 as it did in 1983. The fall in demand was less in this period. Production capacity expanded at a low rate due to reduced investment levels and fewer discoveries. The cost of exploration and development in combination with increased

TABLE 4-8. Crude Oil Supply

	1979	1980	1981	1982	1983 Quota	1983 Actual
OPEC	30.928	26.878	22.358	19.017	17.500	16.137
Saudi Arabia	9.531	9.924	9.624	6.327	5.000	4.263
Algeria	1.194	1.016	.965	.701	.725	.672
Ecuador	.240	.228	.225	.209	.200	.238
Gabon	.196	.177	.152	.155	.150	.160
Indonesia	1.621	1.563	1.605	1.337	1.300	1.224
Iran	3.035	1.490	1.380	2.800	2.400	2.450
Kuwait	2.406	1.706	.941	.671	1.050	.788
Libya	2.075	1.781	1.175	1.246	1.100	1.052
Nigeria	2.301	2.085	1.414	1.298	1.300	1.228
Qatar	.506	.473	.405	.328	.300	.252
U.A.E.	1.824	1.711	1.499	1.250	1.100	1.092
Venezuela	2.356	2.222	2.108	1.895	1.675	1.824
U.S.S.R.	11.700	11.993	12.176	12.250	-	12.464
U.S.A.	8.533	8.647	8.555	8.672	-	8.674
China	2.123	2.114	2.022	2.040	-	2.119
Other Countries	9.188	10.341	11.163	12.168	-	13.039
World Taotal	62.472	59.973	56.274	54.147	-	52.433
Capacity (estimated)	68.750	69.150	69.650	70.100	-	70.175
% Utilization	91	87	81	76		75

sociopolitical risk was a major factor in the oil company mergers that took place during 1983–84. The acquisition of crude oil reserves on the stock exchange was safer and less expensive than in the field.

Scenario for Future Crude Oil Prices

Using the market price for Saudi Arabian light at Ras Tanura as the measure, the forecast is for US$19/barrel by end-1986. In 1987 additional downward pressure will build, and another decline to about US$16/barrel will occur by year-end. If the 1986–87 recession is being called a depression by some advanced nations as well as developing countries undergoing a financial crisis, the price will further decline to new low levels at US$13.50/barrel. Only a small probability exists that OPEC members will be able to maintain discipline. Regardless, a break in crude oil prices is inevitable for the following reasons:

1. Capacity for oil exports outside OPEC is expanding. China, Cameroon, Malaysia, Mexico, Norway, and United Kingdom are examples.
2. Domestic consumption is being increasingly supplied from internal production, thereby taking buyers out of the market place. Brazil, Chile, India, Ivory Coast, and the United States are among several examples.
3. The Soviet Union is supplying oil outside its satellites for strategic goals and to generate convertible currency. Argentina, Greece, Turkey, Vietnam, and Yugoslavia are examples. The Soviets are also supplying petroleum industry technology to several countries to develop internal production.
4. Conservation and substitution to new energy sources have been successful in Europe, Japan, North America, and other locations. Even when economies gain momentum, the surge in demand is minimal. Part of thc success is restructuring away from energy-consuming industry.

It is more probable that discipline will not be maintained within OPEC. The reasons include the following:

1. Some members are overborrowed and are desperate for foreign exchange earnings. As it did in 1984, Nigeria is likely to be among the first to act independently on price and volume when OPEC concessions are inadequate. However, Ecuador and Venezuela are in similar positions, and

Indonesia is drifting into trouble.

2. Saudi Arabia needs about 5.5 million b/d to obtain natural gas for desalinization and electricity generating plants. In 1984 output averaged 4.694 million b/d, and at year-end the country conceded another 150,000 b/d to Nigeria in its role as buffer between demand and supply within OPEC. Currently, budget and current account deficits are forcing repatriation of only interest on investments abroad, but falling crude oil prices and a recession will increase pressure to act more aggressively and avoid spending capital.

3. Iran and Iraq are now seeking ways to increase foreign exchange earnings to fight the war and supply their economies (Iran's imports rose 64% in 1983). A cease-fire similar to the Korea truce is likely during the next rainy season. Currently, the two countries are operating at 45% of estimated capacity and 42% of 1978 production. The need for cash from crude oil in order to rebuild will coincide with the next worldwide economic downturn. This factor alone will destroy price discipline.

4. Radicals have been a disruptive influence within OPEC, ignoring economic principals and giving priority to religious and political ideology. Also, cultures are significantly different within the group, and self-interest will dominate as members are stressed by declining markets.

The OPEC quota has been 16.5 million b/d since October 1984. Production averaged 17.19 million b/d in 1984. During 1986 the quota can be no higher than 15 million b/d. The socioeconomic impact of a decrease in country quotas will be severe and unity of position within OPEC appears impossible.

Two major conclusions emerge from the predicted petroleum supply/demand situation:

1. Developing countries that are net oil exporters and have large populations are now confronted with a serious shortfall of convertible currency. The remainder of the decade will be a financial disaster for these nations. Elaborate development plans formulated on the basis of rising (or at least stable) petroleum prices are being cancelled, but the full realities of the fall in crude oil prices have not yet been considered. Servicing their large foreign debts will be impossible. Increases in oil production will result in price decreases that at least offset the added volume.

Net oil exporters are experiencing a profound structural change in their outlook. Without Part II solutions, most such countries will be in lasting financial trouble by 1987. The Mexican government, for example, has no principal payments in this period, but the country will be unable to pay interest at that time.

2. No significant relief from present crude oil prices will occur until the recession starts in the United States during the second half of 1985. Net oil importers will still be paying more than 50% higher prices in 1987 than they paid ten years earlier. During that decade external debt will have grown to the point at which interest on these loans is a larger item in the current account than imported petroleum. Countries such as Brazil, Morocco, Philippines, Portugal, and others have been irrevocably damaged by the exogenous events of the 1970s. The gains from a recession in lower crude oil prices, lower real interest rates, a realistically valued U.S. dollar, and rescheduled debt service payments will be offset by slow economic activity and low levels of foreign exchange generation. If no global solution is implemented, many more net oil importers will become impoverished. The only answer is to start over again.

REFERENCES

Haner, F.T. *Global Business Strategies in the 1980s.* Praeger Publishers, 1980.

International Financial Statistics. International Monetary Fund, March 1985.

International Issue. *World Oil Magazine,* February 1985.

5

Primary Actors in the Financial Crisis

Some analytical comments on the primary actors involved in the crisis are necessary. The borrowers can be divided into two categories: (1) the developing countries that receive most of the media attention, and (2) advanced countries living beyond the standards justified by the output of their economies. The private borrowers in both types of sovereign states also play an important role, but ultimately they are controlled by the governments under which they operate. Comments on the United States as an international borrower provide background for Part II solutions.

The lenders are more numerous. They include (1) the IMF and other international organizations that provide funds and guarantees, (2) collective groups of creditor countries such as the European Community, the Intergovernmental Group for Indonesia, the Paris Club, and ad hoc emergency coalitions, (3) individual countries providing loans, guarantees, and grants, and (5) smaller banks mostly drawn into international lending in the 1970s. Each of the five categories of lenders has a different perspective as the situation builds to a climax.

A tragedy is being constructed. The comments in the last section of this chapter clarify the constructive role that could have been played by the United States in 1983–84 and how action was delayed because of an election campaign.

THE BORROWERS

The lenders have tended to prefer dealing with democracies in which some form of accountability exists. Authoritarian governments have diverted more of the borrowed funds into private accounts or into applications that are more helpful to key individuals than to economic development. However, capital flight from countries with either category of government has been a major factor in the weakening of their financial structure.

Developing Countries

The theoretical objective of borrowing foreign exchange was to upgrade living standards by building infrastructures and productive facilities that would create new exports and substitute for imports. These new additions to the economy would service the debt incurred through the convertible currency earned and would generate increasingly higher quality jobs. Sociopolitical stability would result from prosperous populations justifiably proud of their accomplishments.

The reality is quite different. Honest miscalculations were made. The demand for commodities slumped and prices fell; thus, cash flow from projects was below expectations. The outlook for energy-related facilities was particularly affected in the 1980s. The desire of leaders to be identified with high visibility projects wasted money. Factories and roads with political pay-out were given priority over more productive investments. Nationalistic decisions were made; heavy industry was installed despite excess capacity around the world. Often corruption was rife. Wealth was accumulated by the elite while economic development lagged behind expectations. The movement of this wealth into convertible currency and out of struggling countries was frequently a crippling blow to solvency.

Most importantly, basic management principles were usually ignored. Loans with medium-term maturities were accepted for projects with very long-term paybacks in convertible currency. Funds were allocated to paying for consumables, thereby laying the foundation for arrears. Contingency planning that allowed for overruns, price declines, slow market penetration, and so forth, was not included in feasibility studies. From the lenders' position, as time passed the assets on the books of banks (loans to foreign parties) to offset obligations to depositors became increasingly worthless.

Democracies

Presidents, prime ministers, and colleagues in elected governments attempt to build constituencies during their term in office and strive to be reelected. Even if an individual is restricted from another term, the person's party seeks to retain power. Consider this ongoing goal in the context of an IMF adjustment program. To obtain financial assistance from this organization—and the step is usually a prerequisite to support from private banks—a country must accept terms that strive to correct excesses in the system. Budget deficits must be reduced. Imports must be curtailed to control current account deficits. Other economic and financial measures are imposed such as devaluations, limits on money supply, and goals for interest rates. As a result of implementing these measures, job formation turns negative, and even people with an income cannot buy goods that had become part of their living standard. Adherence to an IMF adjustment program is political suicide in a democracy.

It might be possible to sell a recession to the public for such a limited time as a single period of three years. Significant progress toward carefully defined goals would be necessary, and a campaign to communicate the value of sacrifices would have to be part of the plan. Export markets would be aggressively developed, and the economy would need to recover late in the third year. Complete financial health would have to be restored over a much longer period; the goal would be to establish realistic attitudes about the living standards attainable with the country's human and physical resources during the three years, and gradually to attain financial equilibrium.

Two obstacles prevent this series of events from occurring. First, a majority of the countries in the world are presently attempting to reduce imports sharply while maintaining or expanding exports. As a result, world trade is contracting in real terms because there are many sellers and too few buyers with convertible currency. Second, for reasons related to endemic corruption, nepotism, vested interests, incompetent bureaucrats, and political factors, optimal selection and use of the limited volume of imports that can be purchased fail to take place. The capacity to produce exports decreases with an IMF adjustment program unless the country depends on a single commodity, such as Mexico's crude oil. Even in this case, PEMEX has been hampered by budget cuts.

One option for the borrower under extreme financial hardship is to repudiate the foreign debt informally through a series of moratoriums and, when finally confronted, to formally declare no intention to pay. This means isolation from credit lines, boycotts, and reversion to barter trade with those countries that retain commercial relations. The impact on most economies would be devastating. A government must decide whether socioeconomic problems associated with isolation or those stemming from an IMF adjustment program are more detrimental to the country.

A bubble of public support for repudiation based on nationalistic fervor would occur. Leaders would be temporary heroes who had acted independently and had struck a blow against "oppressors of the nation." After a few months, however, the unemployed and opposition forces would be on the streets demonstrating, and enthusiasm about defaulting would have evaporated. The increasing frustration of large numbers of people would lead to a change in government either through an election or a coup d'etat. Summarizing, repudiation and an IMF solution produce similar socioeconomic results. Yet, compliance with terms imposed by external forces connotes loss of sovereignty, and politicians will be seeking to avoid this type of accusation. The probability of some leaders choosing repudiation is high.

Argentina is one of the few countries that could make the repudiation decision and not face a long depression. It is self-sufficient in food and could become independent in energy quickly with the help of another country, such as the Soviet Union. Argentina's trade pattern was affected by (1) the Falklands/Malvinas War and embargoes enacted at that time, and (2) lack of fresh credits in 1983–84. These developments forced the country to seek new markets and accelerate discussions of trade based on barter. An adequate industrial infrastructure would help the country to survive. The cost in bankruptcies and unemployment would be high, but a government might survive a struggle against "the centers of international financial power." The signal for repudiation by Argentina has already been given. This is the accumulation of foreign exchange reserves while refusing to pay interest on loans.

Developing Countries with Authoritarian Governments

The political factor is less important to President Suharto in Indonesia, President Mobutu in Zaire, and other governments with single, strong leaders. Austerity policies can be implemented, and opposition can be repressed. Even if imports cannot be purchased because debt service absorbs foreign exchange from exports, the severe social impact can be controlled. People starve; malnutrition is widespread; crime and violence escalate. However, the power structure does not change. If a revolt takes place, the changes rarely involve the lower classes. Exceptions, such as in

Iran and Nicaragua, occur infrequently; and even in these cases, creditors are often paid due to the need for fresh credits.

Many strategically important countries have authoritarian regimes. Examples are Pakistan and Korea (ROK). In Turkey the elected government is backed by a strong presidency that evolved from a military take-over. Mexico's Partido Revoluncionario Instituto has retained power for over 50 years. These governments benefit from concessionary terms, grants, and aid tied to projects of high priority. Convertible currency cash inflow improves and creditors get paid. Extreme situations, as in the Philippines where the population is huge and the economy is in dismal condition, will not be made creditworthy by US$ millions paid for military bases or loans approved on concessionary terms. Nevertheless, the foreign exchange flowing to strategically placed countries favorably affects a borrower's role in the crisis. (Israel is an example of an elected government in this special position.)

If recommended solutions are implemented to avoid a financial collapse, the response of authoritarian governments is likely to be more rapid than that of democracies, which is slowed by the need for consensus before making major decisions. A few actions taken to strengthen economies in the postsolution period will not be correct for the same reasons that poor decisions were made in the accumulation of foreign debt, but tighter supervision of restructured loans will reduce the number of bad investments as a percent of the total. Authoritarian governments could feasibly make a leap in economic progress at the expense of the democracies because of seizing a greater share of world markets in the early stages of recovery.

Table 5–1 gives the total external debt for the 103 developing nations reporting their medium- and long-term loans to the World Bank. Only 13 compile private loans. They are the larger countries, but even so the totals exclude (1) private loans not guaranteed by the government in 90 countries, (2) short-term loans, (3) trade credits, and (4) such miscellaneous obligations as bank deposits in foreign currencies owed abroad. The scope and trend of the numbers give perspective on the problem.

ADVANCED COUNTRIES

As the crisis evolved in Africa and Latin American in 1982–84, lenders looked for safer places to which to extend credit. European countries received commitments under

TABLE 5-1. Medium- and Long-Term Debt of Less Developed Countries (in US$ millions)

	1972	1976	1980	1982	1983E	1984E
Worldwide Total*	115,083	398,452	529,179	658,779	780,850	850,000
Principal	8,548	17,028	39,733	46,808	58,086	63,300
Interest	3,435	9,031	30,697	46,207	49,156	54,500
Total Debt Service	11,983	26,059	70,430	93,015	107,242	117,800
Africa South of the Sahara	11,077	27,207	61,252	75,834	89,883	95,500
Principal	526	1,227	2,572	3,400	6,252	6,200
Interest	234	527	2,055	2,654	3,142	3,750
Total Debt Service	760	1,754	4,627	6,054	9, 394	9,950
East Asia and the Pacific	16,457	42,853	84,633	108,948	129,132	138,500
Principal	1,097	2,499	5,342	6,966	8,125	8,250
Interest	476	1,456	4,316	6,458	6,591	7,500
Total Debt Service	1,573	3,955	9,658	13,424	14,716	15,750
Latin American and Carribean	44,810	101,807	201,560	272,753	323,284	363,750
Principal	4,190	8,699	20,276	23,106	27,385**	32,500
Interest	1,731	4,938	17,153	27,415	29,775**	31,500
Total Debt Service	5,921	13,637	37,429	50,521	57,160**	64,000

North Africa and Middle East	8,710	32,007	66,333	67,857	80,428	84.500
Principal	639	1,299	5,012	6,045	6,655	6,750
Interest	164	603	2,714	3,032	2,993	3,500
Total Debt Service	803	1,903	7,726	9,077	9,648	10,250
South Asia	18,173	29,479	48,553	57,255	67,862	72,250
Principal	557	843	1,168	1,258	1,592	1,850
Interest	341	457	733	878	1,046	1,500
Total Debt Service	898	1,300	1,901	2,136	2,638	3,350
Mediterranean	15,856	30,218	66,848	76,153	90,261	95,500
Principal	1,538	2,461	5,363	6,033	8.076	7.750
Interest	489	1,050	3,726	5,770	5,610	6,750
Total Debt Service	2,027	3,511	9,089	11,703	13,686	14,500

* Debt outstanding in the 103 LDCs reporting to the World Bank in 1983 and published in the "World Debt Tables." Only 13 countries report private foreign debt. During 1972-80 only 98 countries reported to the World Bank and some corrections were necessary.

** Totals have been adjusted to conform with research on the difference between actual payments and scheduled payments.

more favorable terms than fundamentals would indicate. While Belgium, Denmark, France, and Sweden had made improvement in their international balances, the countries were still borrowing money to pay for budget and current account deficits.

Canada recovered to current account surpluses in 1982–84; but greater prosperity added imports in 1985, and the borrowing in U.S. dollars (US$) for international balances resumed. The Canadian total for budget deficits and external debt in Table 5–2 are shockingly high. If the budget deficits are not eliminated under the new government, capacity to service the huge debt will be inadequate and banks will not offer new loans in the last half of the decade. The country will then be confronted with a period of sharply reduced living standards and, potentially, escalating inflation from increased money supply to cover budget deficits in Canadian dollars (C$). This possibility also applies to Australia, which recently has been depending more on loans and less on attracting foreign investment.

South Africa has accumulated debt in the 1980s. Private borrowers have been avoiding high domestic interest rates. Also, the government required credit to defend the rand against capital outflows and pay for current account deficits caused by drought and crop failures, generally low metals prices, and soft international markets for other goods. However, the medium-term future looks bright. Energy imports will cost much less during the 1980s. Gold prices will rise rapidly under the scenario given in Chapter 1 (see also "The United States" below). Political stability along its borders is improving. The internal dissent from blacks under apartheid will always be a negative factor.

The United States

An extraordinary phenomenon occurred in the United States during the 1980s. High real interest rates attracted immense amounts of short-term investments in American securities, mostly government offerings such as Treasury bills. The demand for U.S. dollars resulted in a strong revaluation against other currencies. The consequences were a decline in American exports of goods and services and an increase in imports. The current account incurred major deficits, but capital flows into the country maintained a surplus in the balance of payments (US$2.15 billion in 1983).

The sequence was founded on unprecedented budget deficits and the need to issue US$ billions in government securities under the Reagan administration. Also, upward

TABLE 5-2. Data for Major Borrowers among Advanced Countries (in US$ millions)

	Current Account			Budget Deficit			Reported External Debt		
	1981	1982	1983	1981	1982	1983	1981	1982	1983
Australia	-8,269	-8,509	-5,963	-1,504	-1,004	-6,879	22,034	29,056	38,000
Belgium	-4,155	-2,966	-500	-12,903	-11,882	-10,960	15,237	19,604	21,500
Canada	-4,805	2,398	1,274	-7,991	-18,432	-20,164	81,975	90,625	93,275
Denmark	-1,875	-2,259	-1,313	-3,570	-4,665	-6,014	14,046	17,407	20,229
France	-4,809	-12,171	-5,380	-6,020	-12,804	-27,558	24,032	48,926	65,000
Italy	-8,604	-5,767	-1,106	-46,700	-53,648	-58,155	44,600	52,000	58,000
South Africa	-4,077	-2,904	410	-2,138	-2,231	-3,632	21,277	22,855	24,475
Sweden	-2,662	-3,450	-1,061	-10,176	-9,384	-10,917	24,094	27,350	33,500

pressure on interest rates was sustained, even in the election year of 1984, by public borrowing in competition with private demand for money. Confidence in the US$ and in the United States itself as a safe place, the high real interest rates, and concern about low metal prices created a situation in which foreign investors greatly increased their holdings of American public debt. This increase is seen in Table 5–3.

TABLE 5-3. Federal Government Debt Held by Foreigners

Fiscal Year	Foreign Held Debt (US$ billion)	Average Interest Rate (percentage)
1977	95.5	5.2
1978	121.0	6.5
1979	125.1	8.6
1980	126.4	9.4
1981	135.5	11.8
1982	141.6	12.6
1983	160.2	11.2
1984	174.8	11.6

One complication at middecade was that foreign parties began to need the cash at home for their own deficits. In 1983–84 the withdrawals involved mostly interest that had been reinvested in past years. It is expected that capital will have to be repatriated in 1986–87, and this will reinforce the move from U.S. dollars (US$) described in Chapter 1.

Fears about the American banking system are justified, but the United States is a net creditor nation with immense resources. Large volume conversion from U.S. dollars to assets denominated in other currencies by foreign holders of American debt instruments would stress the financial system, but not break it. Some banks already in trouble because of bad domestic and foreign debts would face bankruptcy. However, the Comptroller of the Currency, the Federal Deposit Insurance Corporation, and the Federal Reserve System would act in concert to provide banks with funds to restore solvency in most cases. These rescue efforts would complicate solving the portion of the financial crisis involving foreign debt, but a nationwide bank panic would be avoided if conversion takes place as expected.

THE LENDERS

The International Monetary Fund

The International Monetary Fund (IMF) has played a critical role in creating the crisis. The organization has provided monies from various loan facilities on a country-by-country basis without making an attempt (or none known to the public through 1984) to conceive a global solution. Acting in conjunction with governments of member countries, the IMF has exerted considerable pressure on privately owned banks to continue lending to countries in financial trouble. Involuntary participation in syndications during 1982–84 has pushed many banks closer to insolvency.

The terms of an adjustment program necessarily cause economic hardship within the borrowing country. Excesses in budget and current account deficits, currency valuation, interest rates, tax structure and collections, and trade regulations are placed on a course of correction. The sudden decrease in imports and government spending has consistently led to unemployment, bankruptcies, and social privation.

IMF terms are logical from a purely financial point of view, but they are causing political instability. Parties in power when austerity is implemented gradually lose popularity, and voters opt for a change in leadership with the first opportunity after a period of adjustment. In a few instances, there has been a move to the right following a period during which socialists conclude an IMF agreement. Usually centrist (moderate) governments make the arrangements; they are replaced by left-of-center parties when unemployment rises. Authoritarian governments accepting an IMF adjustment program consistently require repressive moves to maintain order.

The IMF's position is understandable. The alternative approach involving long-range programs to correct excesses gradually and cause less social shock necessitates more foreign exchange than sources will provide. Measure must fit a time frame in which scarce fresh funds can be loaned to the many countries seeking financial assistance, and these measures must show results. Additionally, the IMF realizes that commercial banks, especially the smaller banks, are becoming more reluctant to support syndications for debtor countries. A long-term corrective program would receive fewer and fewer fresh funds, and the terms required by private banks for restructuring past loans would become more severe. Consequently, the IMF is forced to seek terms that are leading to sociopolitical turmoil.

Other International Agencies

The Bank for International Settlements (BIS) has played a constructive role in handling emergencies during the first half of the 1980s. These technocrats have acted as a catalyst to bring together the central banks involved, suggest functional terms, and provide immediate cash. It is probable that the BIS will be prepared for the coming crisis because public statements by bank executives indicate that they have assessed the situation realistically. This organization is one of the alternatives for administering the loans with borrowing countries after temporary solutions during the 1986–87 emergency.

The World Bank (International Bank for Reconstruction and Development—IBRD) and the International Development Agency (IDA) become involved in specific projects and programs rather than general purpose lending. This is also true for such regional development banks as the Inter-american Development Bank and the Asian Development Bank. The goal of these organizations is to finance infrastructure projects, define training programs, experiment with new methods, and delineate applications of funds. The pay-outs are very long term and should not be funded with standard medium- and long-term loans.

These banks offer low interest rates. Fees are minimal, and grace periods are much longer than for commercial loans. Indonesia, for example, has been a frequent recipient of concessionary credit. The averages for the country's medium- and long-term debt at end-1983 were 9.8% interest, 14.7 years maturity, and 4.6 years grace period. In contrast, the same figures for Brazil were 13.2% interest, 11 years maturity, and 3.1 years grace period. If private loan obligations are considered, the differences are even greater because 27% of Brazil's debt is to private parties, while private loans are only 7% of Indonesia's total. Terms for borrowers not guaranteed by the government are much more costly: Maturities are usually less than ten years, and grace periods of two years are considered generous.

Countries

Governments lend money to other governments in two broad ways. First, they make a bilateral transaction for a variety of reasons, ranging from facilitating a commodity purchase to completing a package involving military bases. Second, a government will join others to assist a nation, such as the

Consortium for Pakistan or the European Community's aid for members, such as Greece and Ireland. In both ways, convertible currency is loaned under terms that are more lenient than commercial bank loans. In a few cases, grants are extended.

An important aspect in lending by countries is the support that they give to international organizations. The member, including the debtors, provide the funds for the IMF, the World Bank, and the regional development banks. Quotas are mostly based on capacity to contribute. In addition, the Group of Ten (actually 11 since Switzerland joined in April 1984) assists the IMF with interim financing when approval processes fall behind cash flow needs. The 11 are Belgium, Canada, France, Germany, Japan, Italy, the Netherlands, Sweden, Switzerland, the United Kingdom, and the United States.

From information in previous sections, it can be determined that Belgium, Canada, France, Italy, and Sweden have accumulated large foreign debts and are no longer net creditor nations. Saudi Arabia has partially compensated for these nations' change in status and has loaned SDR billions to the IMF in the 1980s. In addition to credits for loans to members, countries accept quotas for these organizations' operating budgets. The Group of Ten has also responded to rescue missions mobilized by the Bank for International Settlements when a country nears default on obligations.

Another role for governments is to guarantee loans made by others, usually private lenders. The purpose could be (1) an export credit guarantee, (2) financing for a strategically important project, (3) an inducement for banks to participate in a loan syndication to a financially risky county, or (4) a critical general purpose credit. The guarantee fee of 2% to 3% charged by private banks when they provide this service is sometimes waived by the government agency acting as the guarantor, but a few are evaluated on their profit performance during a fiscal year and a fee is part of the arrangement.

Private Banks

The large banks in the net creditor countries (and some in countries that are now net debtors) have had international operations. For decades they have been lending abroad to both governments and to private parties. Their errors in country risk assessment in the years through 1981 are a major factor in the financial crisis. However, their role as a lead manager in syndications is also important.

Hundreds of banks join together in assembling funds for a maxiloan. The transaction is managed by one or more of the large banks. For example, there are nine lead banks and 350 creditor banks in the rescheduling of the Ivory Coast's external debt falling due in the period through 1985. Sometimes the Bank of America, the Chase Manhattan Bank, and others of this size are creditor banks; and the loan is managed by one or more of the other large banks. The important point is that the lead banks interface with the borrower; the borrower therefore regards these banks as the lender. Information relevant to performance on debt service is controlled by managers of the syndication.

The lead bank has, however, conflicting duties and obligations under this system. The borrower is, effectively, the lead bank's customer, and the banker has an obligation of confidentiality to its customer. If the lead bank knows of potential troubles, it is honor-bound not to disclose that information because the customer's relationship with suppliers, purchasers of the goods and services, and potential creditors would be damaged.

The lead bank's obligation to a syndicate member is exactly the opposite. To the creditor bank, the lead bank has the duty of complete disclosure about the customer, particularly if the information indicates nonperformance. As customer weaknesses developed into moratoriums and rescheduling, questions about unethical behavior were raised by the smaller bankers.

Two misconceptions about lending abroad contributed to the early complacency about the issue. First, loans to satellite countries of the Soviet Union were safe because, even if the satellite could not pay, Moscow would be embarrassed by a default and would make certain that the loan was repaid. A "Soviet umbrella" existed for lenders. The 1981 Polish debt defaults proved that there was no umbrella. Second, sovereign loans were perfectly safe. There had been 11 rescheduling through 1976, but the lender had eventually been repaid. A "countries do not go bankrupt" safety net existed for lenders. What later became clear was that governments could print their own money but not foreign exchange. Convertible currency had to allocated to internal socioeconomic priorities.

How were so many mistakes made? One reason was the motivation generated by the advanced countries that wanted to sell their goods and services to developing countries. These nations needed food, capital goods, and new technology. This trade produced an opportunity for the banks providing financing because they could then make an attractive profit on money from depositors, particularly the oil exporters. Governments encouraged this cycling of funds to developing nations. A fundamental flaw in the system besides the jeopardy to principal was that the deposits were short-term, or certificates of deposits with maturities of six month or less. The loans were medium- to long-term. Therefore, timing on loan repayment did not match the potential liabilities to depositors. A need for large sums of money from such a development as falling crude oil prices could create a bank panic.

The decisions about loans (the rate, how much, to whom, for how long, and other terms) were made largely by the banks' line officers, who were responsible for meeting sales quotas. Their compensation and promotions depended on selling beyond these quotas. Frequently these line officers were territorial or country managers. Generally, they were trained in finance and banking administration, including credit analysis. Very rarely did they have necessary background in macroeconomics and sociopolitical analysis. It appears that capacity to assess country risk did not increase significantly during a long residence in the country.

At headquarters the classic banking attitude toward line and staff affected whose country risk assessment was accepted in the decision-making process. Line officers make money and staff officers cost money. Country risk assessment systems in banks were scarce until the Iranian revolution in 1978–79. Early attempts at analysis were usually informal, and political pressure within the bank prevented staff specialists from confronting line officers with a "do not lend" recommendation. A flurry of interest in political risk assessment followed Ayatollah Khomeini's return to Teheran, and people with expertise but limited business experience were added to forecast this dimension. Other aspects of country risk assessment, such as statistical analysis of economic and financial factors, were not generally integrated into a complete system. In the 1980s (a few in the late 1970s) the lead banks had acceptable systems, but apparently the forecasts were either wrong or ignored.

The smaller banks in syndication, usually regional banks in the United States, could not afford the staff for country risk assessment. Many did not even know that services exist that provide such analyses and forecasts. They depended on the lead banks to provide this information. In retrospect, it would be a very poor salesperson who would place doubts about joining a syndication in the minds of line officers with limited international experience. Consequently, the conflict of interest issue is a major factor in the financial crisis.

LOST OPPORTUNITY

The official position of the United States is that growth in the advanced countries in the 1980s will permit the debtor nations to comply with schedules for principal and interest payments through sales to these expanding economies. Two adjustments are conceded as necessary for success. The debtor nation must carefully control imports and reduce budget deficits, among other measures required to achieve an efficient economy aimed at foreign exchange generation. These are the IMF adjustment programs. Second, debt service must be tailored to capacity to pay, and rescheduling of previously rescheduled debt will be needed in some cases as (1) market conditions change or (2) governments fail to optimize use of resources. For example, in the case of Mexico, falling crude oil prices would require a reexamination of payment schedules.

A classified report titled "Approach to the International Debt Situation—A Policy Overview" was prepared by the U.S. government in 1982–84. It was sometimes called "NSD-3" for National Security Directive 3. Four working groups were organized in 1982. They covered political and security considerations, the impact of international debt on American economic recovery, trade and trade policy dimensions, and alternative proposals for American policy. The stance taken at the London Economic Summit in June 1984 and reiterated subsequently by Treasury Secretary Regan indicates that the administration opted for handling each country individually rather than following the proposal in Chapter 6. The work done for this report and the team assembled to do the analysis will, regardless of the government's present position, be useful in developing guidelines for American action when the crisis culminates.

The United States presumes that the people of a country and its government will dedicate their activity to honoring financial commitments for a sustained period, often for a period of several years. Earlier in this chapter, this dedication was dismissed as highly improbably. Political instability and nationalism will certainly result in repudiation of these commitments. The growth on which it is dependent is also a key factor, and the results of extensive econometric modeling for the American report are discussed below.

Four Econometric Models

The four groups organized in 1982 were composed of highly qualified government technocrats. This team, aided by previous OECD work in building a model of the world economy and by the OECD's "interlink" concept, constructed another world model, which was completed in early 1983. These professional reached consensus on the interrelationships, weightings, and other assumptions that must be made, for instance, the price of crude oil. Data on the scope of debt in many countries would have to be altered if rerun in 1985, as would other details because of what has since occurred.

Several alternatives were narrowed to the following four conclusions:

1. If average real growth for gross national product (GNP) of the 24 OECD countries (plus Yugoslavia) averages 4.2% annually during the 1980s, the debtor nations gradually work out of austerity and remain current on rescheduled debt service. Even if the growth rate is as low as 3%, most of the countries reduce external debt as a percentage of GDP and are generally prompt on principal and interest payments. At the 3% rate, a few countries heavily endebted relative to capacity to generate foreign exchange, such as Bolivia, Chile, and the Philippines, will require special assistance to avoid de facto default. The OECD average growth rate during 1972–82 was 2.5%. During 1980–84 it was 2.3%, aided by American deficit spending.

2. If the OECD average real growth rate is less than 2%, serious trouble develops. External debt will increase as a percentage of GDP, and debt service as a percentage of foreign exchange earned will generally exceed acceptable limits. Inadequate fresh funds will be offered to debtor nations because of poor prospects, and economies will decelerate. This will trigger a series of moratoriums, decreasing resolve to honor international obligations, and a number of large banks writing off loans. The most probable OECD growth rate for the 1985–89 period is 1.5%, assuming prompt action to prevent the financial crisis from becoming a depression. Consequently, lack of leadership in developing a global financial solution by the United States must be based on optimistic forecasts or on secret plans not known to the public to be implemented after the 1984 election campaign.

3. If many countries needing austerity refuse to undertake IMF adjustment programs for the sociopolitical reasons cited in this chapter, the economic and financial

results are chaotic. The model indicates an extreme impact on those banks of creditor nations that are not prepared for large-scale write-offs, particularly in the United States. The austerity in Brazil and Mexico gave Argentina and Venezuela the motivation to resist IMF terms. Also, a loss of sovereignty is implied by compliance in the viewpoint of these highly nationalistic countries. The precedents established by these negotiations laid the foundation for avoiding the dedication to honor external debt obligations.

4. If inflation increases in the 1980s, one beneficial development occurs and a potential disaster is also put in place. The US$ value of the loans will decrease as exchange rates reflect American inflation differentials with other countries and convertible currency earnings rise relative to the face value of the loans. About 15% annual inflation in the United States during 1985–89 is needed for progress and 18% makes significant inroads in the debt by end-decade. However, with 6% real interest rates, the interest component of debt service becomes a crushing burden. Before the U.S. dollar (US$) depreciates adequately, interest rates will be soaring. It is probable that debtor nations will be in de facto default and angry at being forced to pay 21% to 25% interest rates. The best solution is a ceiling on interest charges and negative real rates for an extended period. This could result in Argentina having a lower cost of money than General Motors, but the step would be necessary.

Model One of the four models clearly averts a financial crisis. With sustained growth over 3% in the OECD and ongoing adherence to IMF adjustment programs, the international monetary system is not threatened. The debtor nations undergo a painful economic period with extensive social privation, but obligations to lenders are paid. A few countries require special assistance and repeated rescheduling, but with real OECD growth over 4%, even this is not needed. The probability of Model One is less than 10–90.

IMF adjustment programs generally result in zero growth. They are imposed because the countries are generating inadequate foreign exchange relative to external obligations. One major goal is to reduce imports while at the same time increasing exports to paying and barter customers. Restrictions on imports limit market opportunities for advanced countries and others that have no or fewer financial troubles. The loss of these sales has two impacts: (1) Capacity utilization is lower; investment is concentrated on cost reduction rather than expansion; the outcome is fewer U.S. dollars going to capital equipment and shorter periods of prosperity due to an inadequate investment multiplier; and (2) consumer demand and inventories at all distribution levels tend to become saturated relatively quickly because the rate of job formation is lower and employment requires specialized training in advanced countries. The United States phenomenon in 1983–85 was achieved, as mentioned, through a high level of deficit spending partly funded by short-term investments from abroad.

Model Four could be considered a solution to the potential crisis if (1) the United States would accept a high level of inflation and a lower standard of living and (2) sharply negative real interest rates would be achieved from legislated ceiling on charges. It is doubtful that the American Congress would intentionally escalate prices, devalue the U.S. dollar (US$) (the movement out of the US$ would result from inflation differentials and negative real interest rates), and create operating losses for the banking system (even if offset by subsidies). The steps taken to reduce federal budget deficits will develop downward pressure on the U.S. dollar (US$).

One combination of events that develops a high inflation rate is the additions to money supply needed to rescue several failing banks. The Federal Deposit Insurance Corporation would need large amounts of money to prevent a bank panic, based on the Continental Illinois experience. Budget deficits would be much higher than now anticipated. However, instead of a restrictive monetary policy and foreign capital to help fund the federal deficit, the United States would have to create money. The 18% level is Model Four might be exceeded in this case. If this scenario occurs, and the proposal in Chapter 6 contends that it does not have to happen, nominal interest rates will be 25% or more. This will dishearten the most disciplined adherents to IMF adjustment programs.

Models Two and Three portray disaster. Their probability is high. Real OECD growth during 1985–89 will certainly be less than 2%. Most of the debtor nations will not adhere to IMF terms as the recession deepens in 1986, even if they agree initially, because of sociopolitical implications. Based on this analysis of information revealed to the public about the four models, the classified American government report must have (1) recognized the peril to the international banking system and to the American economy and (2) presented a plan for actions to be taken after the 1984 elections. No other conclusion is logical, given the highest probability forecasts.

Steps the U.S. Government Could Have Taken

The first step would be to acknowledge that (1) the scope of the crisis is beyond a series of individual country rescue missions and (2) profit-oriented private banks must charge a margin over the cost of their money and resulting interest rates will perpetuate the recessions in debtor nations. The interest component of debt service needs to be halved, and the fees for rescheduling, late payments, and miscellaneous services should be eliminated (refer to Chapter 6 for reasons why these points are necessary). This is impossible when private enterprise is seeking maximum earnings from a high-risk borrower.

The next step is to prepare a practical contingency plan. This may have been completed in 1983 as part of "Approach to the International Debt Situation—A Policy Overview," or NSD–3. Assuming that the Reagan administration believed Model One would resolve the crisis, it was imperative to have a specific timetable for "things to do" if it did not. This plan should have two main sections. One should be more detailed than the proposal in Chapter 6 for the technocrats that have to implement the plan. The other is a summary that clearly communicates the major categories of actions to be taken and the reasons why they are necessary to politicians who are most concerned about the impact of the actions on their constituencies.

When a draft of the contingency plan is ready, the details should be discussed with central bank technocrats of other net creditor countries. This may have started in 1983–84 if a contingency plan was a result of NSD–3. Counseling with these governments is critical to (1) include actions that are functionally sound for all parties and (2) develop uniform support for the plan within each government. It is probable that agreement could be quickly reached on general approaches, but different governmental priorities for countries, varying credit exposures, and a range of bad debt provisions could make resolution of details much more complicated and time-consuming. This single factor is a primary reason for writing this book. Hours and days will be important after the crisis culminates, but months will be needed to generate a workable plan.

Congress will be a major obstacle to implementing the plan. Any action plan having the goals of safeguarding the international monetary system and reestablishing economic prosperity will also appear to be a rescue mission for the big banks. An orientation campaign should be carefully prepared that communicates the implications of a global financial crisis for voters in their constituencies as depositors in American banks and as potentially unemployed workers. The contingency plan should contain stipulations for the banks that, while not forcing them into bankruptcy, penalizes shareholders and management for excesses in the lending process. The "pain" imposed on the banks is a pivotal aspect in obtaining congressional approval. The Reagan administration must take the initiative in preparing, amending, and selling the plan. Direct continuous involvement of the Democratic Party will be needed for quick action in Congress.

These steps place the United States in the role of leading the battle to save the integrity of its currency and the mechanism used for international trading transactions. As the largest economy with the most to lose by permitting a financial crisis to happen without intervention, the country should be motivated to take action. Perhaps the political considerations will be put aside in 1986 when a president in his last term is free to implement the plan, if one exists.

6

Recommended Solution

The American economy will decelerate in late 1985 and a recession will be confirmed in 1986 (two consecutive quarters with negative growth). Slower economic activity will cause increasing numbers of (1) bank rescue operations, (2) countries unable or unwilling to make debt service payments, and (3) people sensing a threat to their savings. At that time decisive action will be necessary to prevent a bank panic and subsequent depression.

Organizing a new international bank or extending the authority of the BIS or IMF would take excessive time in an emergency. Bureaucracies achieve consensus on details slowly, more slowly than required to forestall an urgent, impending threat to the financial system. Therefore, central banks must act to save their associated banks from major losses and to circumvent depositor panic. The Federal Reserve System of the United States needs to lead in this effort due to the role of the U.S. dollar in the world economy and because many of its member banks are in serious trouble.

It is important that the technocrats of each creditor country reach agreement on the terms, methods, and procedures to be used and synchronize their actions. This will avoid counterproductive steps that must then be corrected. It is also probable that some central banks will be reluctant to join the American-led rescue effort. Some took steps to prevent overly aggressive lending in the 1970s and to create adequate bad debt reserves in the 1980s. The proposed solution allows for the wide range of jeopardy that exists between Switzerland (zero) and United States (extreme).

Research for this book indicated universal agreement that solutions must involve full payment of principal. A fundamental restructuring of external debt is necessary if the amounts borrowed are not going to be converted to grants, equity in ventures, and bank write-offs. However, in 1985 private banks with profit-oriented shareholders and objectives based on high rates of return on investment:

1. Cannot offer credits at less than the cost of money;
2. Have lost leverage with large debtors, who are beginning to dictate terms for rescheduling; and
3. Face failure as moratoriums on payments require loans to be classified nonperforming.

Only government agencies acting for the collective interests of the public they represent can offer the terms necessary to prevent culmination of the financial crisis in a depression.

PURPOSE OF THE SOLUTION

Europeans, Japanese, and others visualize the American Congress bickering about using taxpayer money to save rich capitalists and greedy bank managers while economies around the world wither. The primary purposes of this chapter are to speed legislative approval required in all creditor countries by proposing the framework of a solution with which to work and, consequently, to save the deposits of voters in the politicians' constituencies. The savings of people in all countries must be protected from bankruptcies, hyperinflation and confiscation.

Preservation of the U.S. banking system and the integrity of the U.S. dollar also preserves the international financial system that has evolved since World War II. It is fundamental that, in the absence of an international currency that can be used for day-to-day transactions by private parties as well as public agencies, the value of the U.S. dollar be as stable as possible in the process of implementing the proposed solution.

Self-interest might also motivate the American Congress. The IMF adjustment programs or voluntary austerity plans underway to correct imbalances in the economies of most developing countries have restricted trade and reduced American exports. If these countries can begin to buy again, several years of pent-up demand will be released. A boom will be created that will be sustained through the 1990s because financial health will have been restored and lessons learned.

Associated with economic recovery are the increased probability for political stability and improved social conditions. Capital investment based on reestablished growth will create new jobs, and people will go back to their old jobs as capacity utilization rises. The conflict between ideologies will remain, and ambition for power will result in nonconstitutional changes in government. Structural unemployment will persist because technology is advancing more rapidly than education and vocational training. Net population growth rates are adding to this problem. Nevertheless, relative prosperity will be restored in most countries, and recruiting people for demonstrations and revolution will be more difficult.

Finally, the process of implementing the solution will assist in correcting imbalances created by the enormous increase in the cost of energy and the recycling of petrodollars. Market forces will establish the price of hydrocarbons because of alternative sources of supply. Application of borrowed funds will be more carefully considered and supervised. Several other factors involved in the building of crisis conditions in the decade after the OPEC price increase will be modified, eliminated, or reduced in scope.

PROPOSED LOAN CONTRACT TERMS

Interest Rates

Near-zero or negative real interest rates will be required. Analysis of the debt service burden in several countries, including such advanced nations as Denmark, indicates that a maximum of 6% can be tolerated. Nominal interest rates higher than 6% begin to create a crisis again. A primary factor in this conclusion is an allowance for business cycles and periods of decreased earnings of foreign exchange. In addition, every point added to 6% lessens economic expansion, international trade, job formation, and so forth, and contributes to sociopolitical instability.

It will be advisable to reward certain countries with rates of 3% or lower. A system should be constructed by the central banks for the 3% to 6% range in which countries could move up or down based on adherence to contract terms. The system could be sufficiently sophisticated to permit a creditor country with strategic priorities to influence the rate applied. For example, the United States has a long border with Mexico, illegal immigration problems, critical trade relations, and sociopolitical reasons for wanting prosperity in that country. In this case, the Americans would have a strong voice in deciding on the annual rate within the range.

Grace Periods

No payment of principal for ten years or more is necessary. Before these payments begin, countries need to construct the foundation for renewed economic growth. The extremes of inventory depletion, low rates of fixed asset formation, capital depletion in industry, infrastructure decay, and inadequate skill levels must be corrected. Many years are involved.

Poorly chosen projects, as previously mentioned, have consumed capital in the past; nationalism, corruption, and changes in external conditions played a role. Governments will need to realign their socioeconomic priorities. A revised industrial profile that considers both internal factors and the international marketplace will have to be established. To be realistic, mistakes will be made again. But some nations will gain form past experiences and leave others behind in the goal of improving the quality of life for their people.

The length of the grace period should be another lever in obtaining adherence to the loan contract. The system might include a range of 10 to 15 years. The length of time permitted would be changed less frequently than the interest rate. All countries should start with the minimum period of ten years. A complication will certainly arise wherein countries adhering to terms need to be rewarded, but countries deviating from stipulations because of special problems (such as coup d'etat, natural disaster, detected large scale corruption, and other situations) also require longer grace periods.

In using interest rates and grace periods as incentives, it is essential to prepare policies and procedures for each combination of circumstances that can be anticipated. Every debtor country should be abiding by the same rules, and the level of discretion should be minimal. Because not every situation will be anticipated, policies and procedures should also be established for handling special situations. Reviews, appeals, and final authority should be clearly stated. This type of work can be completed in the months following implementation of the solution because time will be scarce when the central banks decide that they must act.

Principal Payments

The length of time for repayment should not be less than 20 years, and the choice of 25 or more years would not change the concept. In combination with the grace period, the maturities should be 35 to 40 years. In this way, the principle of full loan repayment is honored, but inflation over such a long period greatly reduces the obligation in real terms. One approach would be to have the same principal repayment period for all countries in order to achieve simplicity and to lower the cost of administration. The variance in overall length of time before the loan is repaid would depend on the grace period. When the time to begin paying principal arrived, structured quarterly (for example) installments would be routine for all debtors. Only the amounts would vary.

Another approach involves introducing another incentive scheme that can be computerized; compliance with terms over a specified period fed into a program communicates the results to debtor and lender, including the interest rate for a year, qualification for grace period length, and payment schedule.

A variation that could be applied to either the structured or the incentive approach is to start with small payments and to increase gradually the amount of principal due each year gradually. Specifically, using a 25-year principal payment period as an example, 4% would be due for 25 years on a straight-line basis. Instead of using this method, the country would start with 1.0% and add 0.25% to the previous year's percentage; the second year would be 1.25% and the last year would be 7.0% of total principal due. This transfers more of the total amount due to the years at the end of principal payment period. The purpose would be to give countries more capital in the earlier years to develop their economies.

The recommended terms are intended to provide cash flow relief to the debtor nations. Therefore, no commitment, rescheduling, late payment, and other fees should be included in the new loan contracts. The incentives should be the means of maintaining discipline (a special "penalty option" explained below is needed for the selected incentives to deal with flagrant cases of violation). A basic principle is that all central banks apply the same terms, policies, and procedures. Agreement should be reached in late 1985 before the crisis culminates so that this part of the solution is ready.

STEP ONE OF THE SOLUTION

The central bank of a country buys with local currency all loan contracts from private or public lenders in that bank's country. Subsidiaries of lenders outside the country are included. Proportional shares are purchased in the case of joint venture banking relationships; the central bank of each partner buys the appropriate portion of a loan contract. This accomplishes two objectives: (1) private banks are removed from dealing with debtor nations, and (2) efficiency is gained by having all loan contracts held by one entity in a country, regardless of original purpose of the credit and the lending party.

This part of Step One will take precious time. Therefore, the following elements in the process of buying the loan contracts will be covered in this section:

1. A system for discounting the face value of the loans;
2. The right of each creditor country to set its own terms for buying the loan contracts;
3. The method of payment, inflationary factors, and the need for valid assets to offset depositor liabilities;
4. Depositor insurance organizations and adequate funding to protect depositors of banks not surviving the crisis; and
5. Eligibility of countries for the new terms, including overborrowed advanced countries.

As part of Step One in the debtor nations, the government takes responsibility for all external debt, public and private. The central bank (preferable to the ministry of finance) then requires each borrower to sign a new loan contract obligating payment for the outstanding principal amount converted to the local currency. Terms should be similar to the terms being offered by the creditor country central banks. The IMF should act as the moderator in this process so that no irregularities, political favoritism, or unfair penalties take place. The objectives of this process are to have these loans be very long-term liabilities on the financial statements of borrowers and to have minimal impact on local currency cash flow in the years following the solution.

Loans that have been extended by such international

organizations as the IMF, World Bank, regional development banks, and others are converted to identical terms as those offered by the creditor country central banks. A committee of the Club of Ten should act as the focal point for resolving problems arising from this major change in terms, such as budget shortfalls.

At this stage, bilateral transactions can be made between the central banks of creditor countries and debtor nations. Figure 6–1 illustrates the concept. No negotiations are involved. Even the interest rate is assigned, as discussed below. All parties have sufficient incentive to sign contracts involving the common terms.

Figure 6–1. Arrangements within Creditor Countries and Debtor Nations

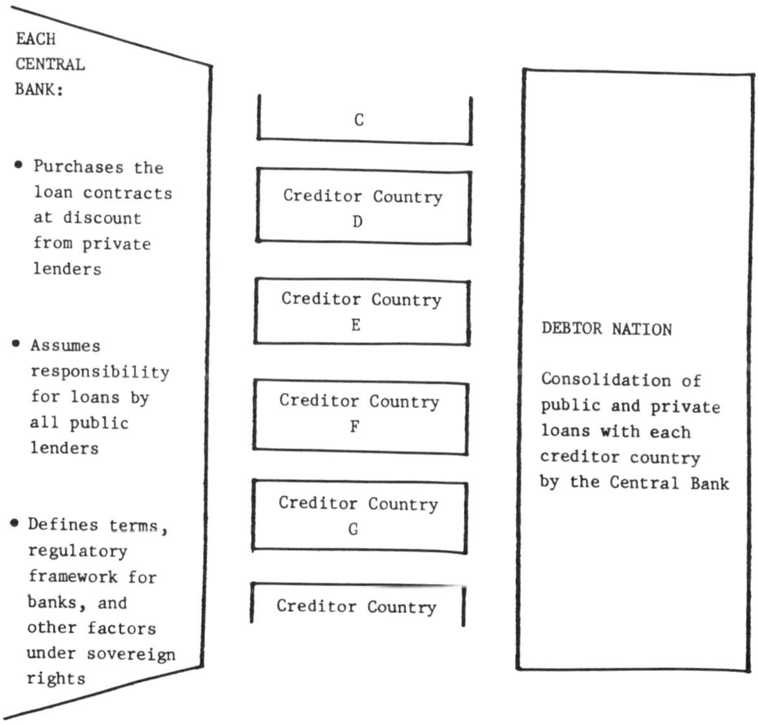

Determining the Discount

Two factors are involved in determining the discount. First, a consensus exists among the general public, banking technocrats, the American Congress, and others that (1) high, perhaps excessive, levels of profits have been earned by the banks from loans in developing countries; (2) the ambition of line officers and the incentives given them to place loans overrode contrary recommendations by staff personnel and professional services; and (3) a penalty must be imposed for the problems that have resulted from this lending process.

Each representative in the lower house of the U.S. Congress must face reelection every two years. Not one of these individuals wants to be identified as a person who saved the shareholders and management of the major banks that have excessive credit exposure in foreign countries. Yet, none want voters in their constituencies to lose their deposits as a result of inaction. The prudent middle ground is to devise a system for discounting the loans and exacting a significant penalty from the banks. To clarify, a loan contract stating that the borrower owes US$100 million would be purchased at 60% or 75% of this value, not 100%.

Second, technical factors justify a discount. The banks are freed from high-risk loans, the possibility of failure in some cases, and the management time and expenses incurred to chase interest and principal. Moreover, the interest received is likely to be less than the cost of money, and decades will pass before recovery of principal takes place. In addition, an ongoing risk will exist that debt service will not be paid even under the proposed terms. A market has developed for discounting the loans in overborrowed countries, but the rates are probably not indicative of what should be used for a global system.

Several methods of determining the discount rate are possible. The key point is that the approach selected should leave very little to qualitative judgment. A mechanical approach will reduce the bickering and accelerate the administrative process. Table 6–1 gives an example. The Lenders Risk Rating (LR) is obtained from BERI S.A.'s FORELEND service and details on the methodology are given in Appendix B.

A relationship exists between the degree of discount and the interest rate to be charged. A country deserving a low discount rate will probably merit a low interest rate. Referring to Table 6–1, France and Taiwan (ROC) would qualify for the minimum discount and the 3% interest rate. Mexico has followed IMF economic and financial guidelines and has succeeded in most categories. In addition, the country has strong recovery potential after the solution's implementation; both the discount and interest rates would

TABLE 6-1. Sample Method of Discounting Loan Contracts

Countries	Basic Risk (Nonpayment, delays, expediting expenses) 60%	Presence of and Adherence to an Adjustment Program 40%	Weighted Total 100%
United Kingdom	0	1	0.4
Taiwan (ROC)	1	1	1.0
France	2	1	1.6
Denmark	3	1	2.2
Belgium	3	2	2.6
Australia	2	4	2.8
Canada	2	4	2.8
Ireland	4	1	2.8
Sweden	3	3	3.0
Spain	4	2	3.2
Malaysia	3	4	3.4
Algeria	5	2	3.8
Korea (South)	4	3	3.8
Greece	4	4	4.0
India	5	3	4.2
Portugal	5	3	4.2
Turkey	5	3	4.2
Mexico	6	2	4.4
Colombia	5	4	4.6
Israel	5	4	4.6
Thailand	5	5	5.0
Egypt	6	4	5.2
Nigeria	6	4	5.2
Chile	7	4	5.6
Indonesia	6	5	5.6
Brazil	8	3	6.0
Venezuela	6	6	6.0
Philippines	7	5	6.2
Argentina	8	8	8.0
Zaire	9	8	8.6

Key: 0 = Best Case; 10 = Worst Case.

Discount Formula: 100%--(Weighted Total x 5%) = % of Loan Contract Paid to Lenders. Example--Mexico: 100%--(4.4 x 5%) = 78% Paid by Central Banks to Lenders with Loan Contracts in Mexico. Example--Brazil: 100%--(6.0 x 5%) 70% Paid by Central Banks to Lenders with Loan Contracts in Brazil.

Recommended Source of Data: Basic Risk--Computer program uses published and classified data in ratios and interrelationships to estimate a country's credit worthiness. Adjustment Program--Panel of experts render qualitative judgment through ratings of criteria portraying conditions.

be in the middle part of the scale, whereas such countries as Argentina and Zaire would merit the 6% interest rate and near maximum discounting of loan contracts. Step Two refers to Table 6–1 in giving examples of terms extended to debtor nations.

Rights of Creditor Countries

No limits are placed on a country in dealing with lenders within that country. Logic suggests that the face value of loan contracts be discounted, that regulations permit the banks to lend to foreign parties again, and that other dimensions of the buy-out and restructuring establish a healthy and profitable financial community. However, the taxpayers of a creditor country may want some form of special tax levied to compensate for government revenues used to implement the global solution. Each country must be free to determine the details affecting its banks and public agencies and not be bound by the actions of other countries.

Private banks are adding to bad debt reserves as rapidly as cash flow will permit. The collective exposure of Swiss banks is much less than that of other creditor countries, and most Swiss banks have 100% reserve coverage. Resolution of nonperforming foreign loans in the manner described in this chapter will release those funds for banking operations. However, the Swiss government may identify the need for regulations that will be unique to Switzerland.

Some countries will be creditors on one hand, and debtors on the other. Belgium and France are examples. Other examples will stem from trade credits that have accumulated. Operating companies and others will be seeking payment under their government's buy-out program. Most countries will permit participation of nonbanking organizations to clear the way for future trade. Special circumstances will certainly develop, however, that will require exclusions.

Method of Payment

Loan contracts are assets on the financial statements of lenders that are not governmental agencies. Something must substitute for these assets because they offset the liabilities to depositors and other debits on the books. However, full payment in cash is not logical because this level of sudden liquidity would create (1) higher inflation, (2) huge federal budget deficits, and (3) a stampede by the banks to find borrowers for the funds. Stresses on the financial structure of creditor countries would be excessive.

The right of a government to devise its own solution applies. Therefore, the following suggestions are made to assist those responsible for designing a specific method of payment:

1. *Initial cash payment.* The financial health of many banks may be in jeopardy. It is probable that cash will be required for 20% to 25% of the discounted value of the loan contracts in the first year to provide adequate liquidity as the crisis develops. Furthermore, government-issued notes maturing in the second year may be necessary to provide more cash. Therefore, up to 40% of the total payment may be needed within 24 months to secure the stability of the banking system.

2. *Securities with Graduated Maturities.* Regardless of the percentage remaining of the discounted value of loan contracts, creditor countries must issue instruments that are a financial responsibility of the government. This provides the needed assets for the banks and strengthens the financial statements of companies selling trade credits. However, these long-term obligations should mature in successive years to avoid a stress on the federal budget at a specific time. An example is having 5% coming due every year, starting with the sixth year after the initial purchase; if 35% had been paid in the first two years, 5% would come due every year during years 6–18.

3. *Interest Rate on Outstanding Amounts.* The critical question is whether or not the government wishes to pay more than it receives. A 3% to 6% interest rate range has been suggested for sovereign borrowers. A fixed rate on the securities does not appear to be prudent because the amount of interest actually received will vary with the performance of the debtor nations. One solution is to have the weighted average interest rate paid in a year by all debtor nations be the rate paid to sellers of the loan contracts.

Depositor Insurance

The American banks are in fragile condition from having more nonperforming loans, domestic and foreign, than is desirable. Japanese banks are heavily exposed in developing counties, but are adding reserves against default more rapidly than the Americans. In contrast, the German and Swiss banks have nearly 100% reserves against bad debts abroad. A spectrum of depositor jeopardy is created by comparing the probabilities of banks failing when the financial crisis unfolds.

The Federal Deposit Insurance Corporation (FDIC) in the United States will require large amounts of cash to perform the series of rescues that are going to be needed. Some banks, large and small, will not survive and their depositors will need reimbursement. Therefore, in addition to cash for purchase of loan contracts, the American Congress will have to legislate funds for the FDIC. Large deficits in the federal budget are a certain result, even if a bank's fee for depositor insurance is increased substantially as part of the rescue process. It is also probable that inflation will be double digit (12% to 15%) as a result of the cash injected into the system. Consequently, real interest rates will be negative for a period until the economy generates demand for loans from private borrowers.

Eligibility of Countries

All countries should be included in the solution. Labels such as advanced, industrialized, developing, less developed, communist, and so forth, should be eliminated. The proposed process will allow separate organizations within the central bank to handle (1) creditor relationships with other countries and (2) debtor obligations. Computer software to determine the current and future net position on receipts and payments and to offer alternative actions will enable the executive in charge of the two organizations to be informed and guide the decisions of his subordinates.

Lenders must not be allowed to choose loans that they wish to exclude from the solution. Attractive interest rates, certain repayment, personal relationships, strategic plans, and many other reasons will be offered to place loan contracts outside the solution. The concept will function if this occurs, and the rights of sovereign countries under the solution give governments the option of letting their banks exclude loans, but it is best to avoid the complications that will arise as a result of the exclusions.

Architects of the solution within each country should attempt to avoid all time-consuming alternatives. A structured simplicity is desirable. Thousands of banks, public agencies, and companies will be involved. Clear guidelines based on near-zero deviations from the basic framework will reduce the time consumed, increase the efficiency of everyone, and minimize opportunities for corrupt practices. In addition, the coordination between central banks will be easier if the policies, procedures, and practices do not vary widely. The BIS could act as intermediary between countries, communicating problem solving ideas, suggesting simplifications, and expediting as required.

STEP TWO OF THE SOLUTION

The creditor countries must now deal with the debtor nations. Figure 6–2 is an extension of Figure 6–1. New loan contracts must be signed by the central banks.

The suggested loan contract terms have been identified in this chapter.

Figure 6–2. Signing of Consolidated Loan Contracts with Central Banks

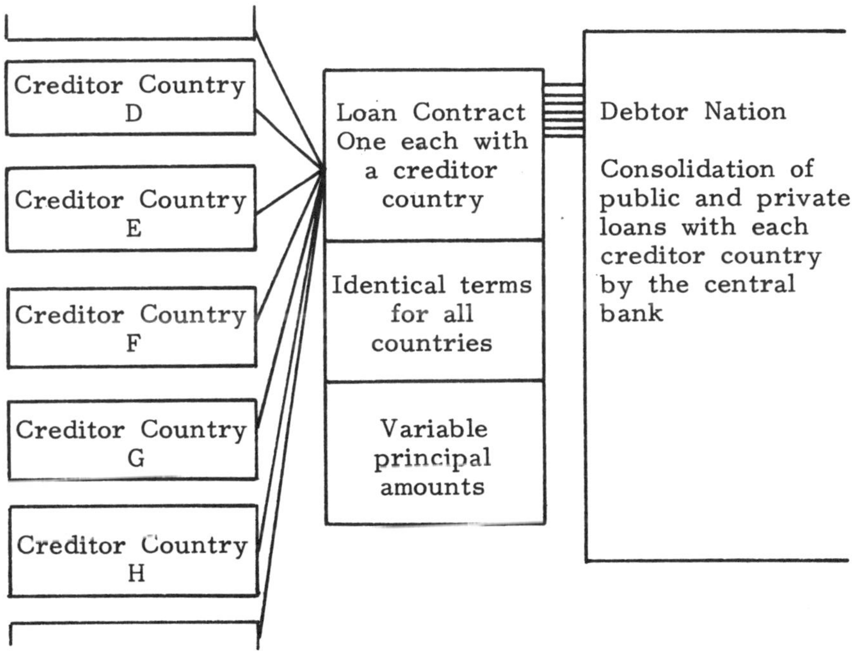

The debtor nation is responsible for the face value of the loan contracts purchased from the lenders, not the discounted amount. For creditor countries, it is logical that each central bank consolidates the hundreds of loan

agreements into a single contract with an addendum listing the loans involved. This procedure should be universally accepted to reduce time lost to bureaucratic delays.

The debtor nation will review and confirm the list. Discrepancies can be verified through the original loan documents. It is probable that borrowers, public and private, will neglect to reveal some foreign debt. The scope of the solution process is so large that clerical errors will take place. This phase will take months, not weeks, and patience will be a scarce commodity at the end of the verification and contract signing period.

Clarifying what happens in Step Two, the central bank of a debtor nation signs as many agreements as there are countries to which the debtor nation owed convertible currencies. A date must be specified that is at least 30 days before the beginning of the verification and contract signing period. This date is important because a clearly stated moment in time is needed to define credits covered under the buy-out and restructuring program and those transacted after the specified date that have normal terms. World trade cannot stop while the technocrats are implementing the solution. In fact, as confidence builds that a solution is actually going to take place, trade will accelerate, and international banking will be functioning freely as a result of Step One.

Loan Contract Currency

Denominating the new agreements in U.S. dollars is a mistake that should be avoided. Budget deficits, high real interest rates, and strength of the American economy have been primary causes of a strong U.S. dollar. The impact on parties in other countries with U.S. dollar-denominated debt service has been extremely damaging. No progress in budget deficits is possible when both the scale of the buy-out program and the bolstering of the FDIC is considered. Progress made toward budget cuts and increased revenue in 1985 will be overwhelmed by these two needs for federal funding. Consequently, the U.S. dollar should not be the loan contract currency.

A basket of currencies is better than using one currency. It is appropriate for a global foreign debt solution to have a valuation of amounts due that is not dependent on a single country's influence. The Special Drawing Rights (SDR) computation is weighted by the U.S. dollar but also includes the French franc, German mark, Japanese yen, and British pound sterling. The SDR is superior to other baskets of currencies that omit the U.S. dollar and is, therefore, a strong candidate for the loan contracts.

A new currency unit is the best solution. In 1981 the SDR changed to the five countries instead of the 16 included during the 1974–80 period. Those 16 countries may not be the optimal choice in 1986, but a broader base than five nations is desirable. The SDR concept of choosing the countries with the largest exports of goods and services is probably too narrow in the context of debt service. Regardless, experiments with data on 1980–84 currency performances, real interest rates, and debt service obligations would yield an optimum basket.

Interest Rates

The suggested terms involve the same grace and principal payment periods for all debtor nations at the outset. Both could be used as reward mechanisms for prompt or early debt service payments. Interest rates would not be the same. They would start at different levels and move up and down more frequently than changes in the grace and principal payment periods.

How do the central banks choose the appropriate interest rate? Table 6–1 gives a sample method for discounting the face value of loan contracts. It identifies the relative level of risk exposure; a rating system similar to this should be constructed and used for both discounting and interest rate determination. Such a scale, Table 6–2, is derived from Table 6–1.

TABLE 6-2. Guide to Interest Rates

Rating (Weighted Total)	Interest Rate	Microscale Rating (Weighted Total)	Microscale Interest Rate
0.0 - 2.0	3.00%	2.2	3.1%
2.1 - 3.0	3.01 - 3.50	2.4	3.2
3.1 - 4.0	3.51 - 4.00	2.6	3.3
4.1 - 5.0	4.01 - 4.50	2.8	3.4
5.1 - 6.0	4.51 - 5.00	3.0	3.5
6.1 - 7.0	5.01 - 5.50	3.2	3.6
7.1 - 10.0	5.51 - 6.00		

Out of the thirty countries rated in Table 6–1 only France, Taiwan, and United Kingdom merit the lowest rate of 3% at the beginning. Using the microscale, Belgium would pay 3.3% and Spain 3.6%. At the other end of the spectrum, the Philippines would pay 5.1%. Argentina and Zaire would pay the maximum amount o 6%. Mexico would benefit from adherence to an IMF adjustment program and would pay 4.7%. Under the "strategic importance" rule, the United States might be permitted to reduce the interest rate 10% of the amount derived from the scale. Therefore, Mexico would pay 4.23% in this example. Japan could make the same decision for Korea (South), and so on.

A rating system for countries will minimize the arguing about the rate to be paid by a country. It will also assist the process of securing agreement between creditor countries on a uniform schedule of terms. Considerable discussion will occur about who will design the system, its structure, and the discount and interest rate scale. An independent organization such as the BIS is probably the best starting point for the preliminary design, followed by a creditor country working session to resolve points of dispute. Situations involving "strategic importance" should be identified in this session.

At the conclusion of the verification and loan contract signing period, the debtor nations will have low annual foreign exchange commitments in debt service. For at least ten years, only interest will be paid, and the rate will be low. For example, using round numbers, Brazil's US$100 billion external debt would cost US$5 billion/year instead of over US$14 billion. As a result, the current account could be in balance despite heavy purchasing abroad for inventory replenishment, and the country's economy could begin to expand. Caution about funding this expansion and the recovery in the other debtor nations is necessary so that debt does not accumulate again at a rapid rate.

Step Two could involve secretive relationships between creditor and debtor countries that should not take place. Concessions on interest rates and guaranteed additions to the grace period could be offered for a favored trading position. Mining rights, fixed prices on commodities, and other arrangements interfering with the free functioning of the marketplace could be negotiated. Therefore, it is advisable to have an IMF technocrat from a third country present in all discussions. The possibility of irregularities being reported will minimize the number of these situations. However, the IMF technocrat cannot be with the parties at all times, and secretive relationships will occur in Step Two.

STEP THREE OF THE SOLUTION

Culmination of the financial crisis and the need to implement a global solution will occupy the politicians, bureaucrats, bankers, and others for at least twelve intensive months. Time lost to indecisiveness will extend the period, if there is no preparation in advance. Consequently, resolution of some problems will be postponed to the time after the signing of new loan contracts. Some of these cases are discussed below.

Lending by International Organizations

Fresh money (convertible currency) will be needed by countries for working capital as recovery becomes feasible. Old debt will be restructured, but the 1986–87 recession will have kept foreign exchange generation and international reserves at low levels. However, many of the private banks will be cautious about new credit exposure abroad, particularly in debtor nations receiving large discounts and relatively high interest rates when the solution is implemented. A period of many months will pass before banking and business gain confidence, and momentum for economic growth would be lost without fresh money at concessionary rates.

It is proposed that the IMF and World Bank receive a special allocation of funds from the Group of Ten nations. This convertible currency would be in the form of 12- to 15-year loans to be repaid on a schedule similar to that which the countries receiving the money would be paying the IMF and World Bank. IMF funds would go to general purpose needs, such as inventory replenishment. World Bank money would be for projects such as infrastructure rehabilitation (not new schemes). A spread between the interest rate that is charged borrowers and a lesser rate paid to Group of Ten nations would cover the expenses of administering receipts and payments involved in the proposal.

The amounts provided by the IMF should fit a formula such as the average for 15 days of import coverage during the 1983–84 period. Project funding would be based on priorities, and the convertible currency component would be detailed in each project. Because companies might be reluctant to ship goods or provide services if payment is to be made by the debtor nation, it would be prudent to have mutually approved invoices (by the country and the IMF or World Bank) paid by the international organization. Alternatively, the IMF and World Bank could make their guarantee of payment necessary on each invoice and gain the right of review for items being purchased. This will also prevent any misuse of funds.

Cartels

Creditor countries have gained a means of maintaining supply and demand as the basis of pricing commodities, including crude oil. International cartels and monopolies should be illegal. Demand for raw materials will be rising at end-decade, and prices should be a function of supply in relationship to this demand. No "OPECs" should be permitted to form regardless of commodity, and organizations of this type should be disbanded.

Separate from the "flagrant debtor nation" penalty involving sharply higher interest rates and shorter grace periods, a "criminal debtor nation" penalty should be established for countries that attempt to form cartels or monopolies with other countries. The loan contracts should have clauses that permit either of the two penalties to be invoked. The "criminal debtor nation" penalty should be severe, for instance, 20% interest, no grace period, and automatic conversion to a medium-term maturity. It will be difficult to establish a cartel if debtors concur in the loan contract and a financial penalty is involved that could outweigh the benefits of higher prices.

Such grower organizations as those for coffee and sugar should be permitted to function. Their goals should be orderly supply through quotas, adequate inventories in the case of natural disasters, and price supports to prevent hardship for farmers. When any international organization changes from avoiding oversupply and price declines to creating undersupply and price escalation, the creditor countries would have the right to invoke the "criminal debtor nation" clause.

The dismantling of "OPECs" should begin with the completion of Step Two. One of the international organizations could be charged with this responsibility. This organization could also monitor developments and arbitrate if an "association" begins to constrain the free market.

Special Country Situations

Iraq

The country has received about US$37 billion in aid from Gulf Cooperation Council (GCC) states, particularly Saudi

Arabia. These transfers have been called loans. It is highly probable that they are grants, not true financial obligations of Iraq. One objective of the recommended solution is to eliminate financial situations such as this. The creditworthiness of every country involved is affected. Iraq's position would be much improved and terms could be adjusted for the new perspective on risk. The negative impact on the GCC states is not significant, but the countries' assets would be decreased.

Communist Countries

Some centrally planned countries will be part of Steps One and Two. All are eligible. Yugoslavia, as a member of the OECD in deep financial trouble, will participate from the beginning. It is probable, however, that the Soviet Union and such conformist nations as Bulgaria, Czechoslovakia, and Mongolia will wait to see what happens. This will also be the case for North Korea and Vietnam. Soviet satellites likely to join initially would include Cuba, Hungary, Poland, and Romania.

Data from centrally planned countries do not always match the IMF reporting format. Some are members, but statistics are incomplete. Hungary has made a special effort to provide Western creditors with current account information, foreign debt details, and other relevant data. Generally, adequacy and reliability of statistics from communist countries are problems. This makes attaining comparability with other debtor nations in the discounting and interest rate determination difficult. BERI S.A. has experimented with computer programs to achieve a quantitative assessment of creditworthiness, and rough comparability can be achieved. An array similar to Table 6–1 is needed for these countries, and the BIS should attempt this in parallel with the system used for noncommunist countries.

Excluded Countries

When Step Two is completed, creditor countries should attempt to bring debtor nations outside the solution under the standard terms. This group could include noncommunist countries that were slow in completing arrangements that would permit consolidation, verification, and signing. In a few cases, irregularities will arise that will require time to resolve. Completing Step Three will probably consume a few months in some cases, and 1 to 2 years for others, although the progress being made by countries operating with minimal foreign exchange problems will be a strong motivation to complete outstanding requirements.

STEP FOUR OF THE SOLUTION

When the emergency is over and trade is increasing, creditor countries will want to establish an international agency (called IA below) that handles the loan payments from debtor nations. Rather than creating a new bureaucracy, a department in the BIS seems to be an ideal solution for this responsibility.

The advantages of having an IA instead of individual countries administering their loans are (1) one international bureaucracy is less expensive than one in each creditor country; (2) efficiency in monitoring debtor nation performance is greatly increased because one organization has all the information; (3) expediting and levying penalties is done by an organization other than the creditor country, thereby minimizing the number of situations in which other initiatives are jeopardized by the debt problem; and (4) irregularities and deviations from standard terms are reduced in number because an IA is administering the details.

Two alternative approaches to establishing the organization are possible:

1. *Administrative Functions Only.* In the first approach, the IA provides only administrative services. It collects the money from the borrower and disburses the funds to the lenders. When expediting is needed, IA technocrats apply the incentives created through grace periods and interest rates. When a "flagrant debtor nation" penalty is appropriate, it brings recommendations to a creditor country organization, such as a committee of the Group of Ten.

A supplementary function would be to have analysts who would continuously review the data and identify future payment problems with individual countries and common problems related to the marketplace, natural disasters, technological changes, and similar developments. The IA would also perform services for other international agencies, such as the IMF. It could, for instance, collect and disburse funds on their behalf, because this agency would be administering all aspects of the buy-out and restructuring solution. Care is needed to be certain that performance on the old loans is not jeopardized by new proposals made to these organizations by debtor nations.

2. *Lender of Record.* The IA buys the loan contracts from creditor countries either at face value or at discount.

If the purchase is at face value, the terms for installment payments of interest and principal from the IA to creditor countries must be adjusted to permit the IA to have an operating budget, that is, a margin between funds received from debtor nations and obligations paid to creditor countries provides cash for expenses. If the purchase is at discount, a similar goal is achieved. A lower level of interest and principal is due to the creditor country while debt service from the debtor nation remains the same after the IA buys the contract.

The IA would perform most of the same functions previously mentioned for the alternative in which it is solely an administrator. Its decision-making powers would be increased because the organization would be directly responsible for debt service performance. Even its budget would depend on the foreign exchange received from debtor nations. No committee of the Group of Ten would be involved in disciplinary actions. When the IA's cash flow is threatened, the organization would act to protect itself.

The advantages of the lender of record approach are: (1) the IA functions less like a bureaucracy and more like an efficient financial firm; (2) creditor countries are fully removed from interaction with debtor nations, and fewer conflicts would occur over past debts; (3) budgets of the IA are less likely to balloon than when performing services and receiving revenue contributions from creditor countries; and (4) arguments between sponsors about nationality, language requirements, and background of personnel in the IA are avoided because it will make the employment decisions.

It is probably better to establish the IA as the lender of record. At the beginning, this approach is more complicated because of the legalities in changing hundreds of contracts. The process of setting up the organization will be expensive and time-consuming. Thereafter, the advantages outweigh the disadvantages when comparing it to the purely administrative approach. Time would not then be a constraint, and the added costs would be offset during the life span of the loans.

BRIEF SUMMARY

The international agency (IA) should be organized at the end of 1986 following the American elections. Staffing could be completed in the first half of the year, and many of the details mentioned in this chapter could be resolved before the general public understands the magnitude of the crisis.

Central banks of creditor countries could reach agreement on standard terms, performance incentives, and other variables. Debtor nations, often burdened with incompetent bureaucracies, would have lead time to begin the tasks of taking responsibility for loans denominated in a foreign currency, converting them to local currency loans, and consolidating the obligations by country of origin for new contracts with the IA or creditor countries.

This preparation would greatly reduce the time lapse between the moment a decision is made that a global solution is necessary and the day when it is fully implemented. A clear understanding of what must be accomplished and the costs of delays would create motivation within every organization involved. The IA would be ready for the series of actions that it and the creditor countries must take.

The solution proposed in this chapter assumes that politicians and bureaucrats will wait until there is a crisis that threatens the international monetary system. The Mexican situation in 1982 frightened many people, but only one country was involved at the time and a recovery from recession was clearly underway in 1983 when a banking crisis was a major issue in the media. At the outset of 1985, most of the decision makers apparently believe that country-by-country solutions will circumvent the crisis. However, in 1986 several debtor nations will be causing a financial crisis and a recession will be underway. It will be this type of catastrophe that will prod politicians into action.

7

Alternative Solutions

The fundamentals with which the designer of a solution must work include the interest rate, terms related to principal payments, limiting the number of bank failures, administration of the transition to and operation of the solution, and details associated with fees, economic and fiscal stipulations required of the debtor nation, and public and private portions of the debt. The concept must also consider both the creditor's and debtor's perspective.

Objectives of attempting a solution were stated in Chapter 6. Briefly, they are:

1. Avoid the direct financial consequences of multiple country defaults, which potentially include bank failures, loss of depositor savings, additions to federal budget deficits, weakening of the international banking system, and radical changes in exchange rates.
2. Avoid the socioeconomic consequences of these defaults, which include reductions in global demand based on capacity to pay, business failures, political instability, and such other effects as inflation and extreme unemployment.
3. Create the basis for sustained economic growth by permitting adequate capital for investment and job formation in addition to debt service, and by structuring the solution in a way that reduces the number of countries repeating the decisions that led to the crisis.

During 1982–85 the approach was to postpone principal payments through rescheduling, which delayed recovery of the capital for many years. Interest arrears have been directly capitalized and added to total debt or new money has been loaned to pay past due and current interest obligations. In most cases, countries are being required to dedicate large portions of their foreign exchange earnings to debt service rather than internal growth. This has meant lower living standards for the countries accepting austerity. Wealth is being concentrated in advanced countries, and violent political reactions to the process are taking place.

The next downturn in the business cycle should end the use of this approach. The critical goal has been to avoid technical default and threats to bank solvency. For this to occur, the bank examiners, particularly American officials, must regard payment performance as sufficiently satisfactory to judge the loan contracts as valid assets to offset depositor liabilities. When interest cannot be paid in 1986 or 1987, the banks have the option to do what they have been doing: capitalizing the arrears and adding to debt, or lending more money to pay the arrears. The scope of the problem at that time seems to preclude such an approach. Yet, a probability exists that the United States government will insist on more of the same instead of striving to achieve the three objectives.

This alternative is unacceptable and will lead to depression. Other possibilities exist in addition to the recommended solution or as variations and supplements to this solution.

ALTERNATIVE 1: EXPANDED CREDIT

The concept integrates some of the ideas that have been suggested by analysts and that have been included in other solutions discussed in this chapter:

1. Dynamic economic growth on a global scale will generate the foreign exchange that would permit debtor nations to meet debt service obligations without jeopardizing sociopolitical stability. The OECD average should be no less than 4% for a full decade to accomplish the objectives.

2. Multiyear rescheduling that offers a grace period of several years and that stretches principal payments over two decades would facilitate economic growth. The debtor nations would have additional capital for expansion and job formation as well as complying with debt service obligations.

3. American budget deficits and high interest rates are likely to persist. New credits to generate a surge of prosperity and to override the cyclical factors now causing

a downturn in the business cycle should be in a newly designed SDR that reduces the importance of the U.S. dollar (US$). Responsibility for administering the new SDR (SDRn) would be assigned to the BIS or IMF.

4. Portions of medium- and long-term existing loans and certain short-term maturities could be converted to SDRn credits. The interest rate would be reduced, and average maturities would be lengthened, further reducing debt service pressures.

Where does the BIS or IMF get the many billions of SDRns? Creating an exchange rate from a basket of currencies is different from establishing an international currency that is acceptable to private lenders, suppliers, and contractors. Yet it can be done. The proposal described below is designed to solve the financial crisis rather than create a currency to be used in day-to-day international trade.

1. The source of wealth is property, commodities, industrial assets, and human creativity. Bureaucrats in an international organization can establish a currency only by turning to parties that have such wealth.

2. The Group of Ten (now 11, including Switzerland) has the wealth to back the SDRn in currency form. However, a broader asset base is advisable, both financially and psychologically. An associate group led by China, Norway, and Saudi Arabia should be formed.

3. Debtor nations are issued SDRn credits for both fresh money and conversion of some existing debt. Each country's situation would be tailored to a combination of need, past performance, and specific development proposals. IMF teams would negotiate the terms, although the Group of Ten and associates could establish tight guidelines.

4. Debtor nations would issue SDRn checks and make SDRn transfers to pay lenders, suppliers, and contractors. There SDRns can be used to pay amounts outstanding to sovereign entities only. Banks can extend new loans in SDRns to sovereign borrowers. SDRns are an acceptable component of a debtor nation's foreign exchange reserves.

5. Lenders, suppliers, and contractors could be paid in another currency, either at the discretion of the country or by specification in the loan or sales agreement. It is probable that private parties willing to accept SDRns would have a competitive edge.

6. Suppliers and contractors needing a currency other than SDRns could go to banks authorized by the BIS or

IMF and make the exchange. These banks could also trade in SDRns with other banks, both selling for loan transactions and buying to provide other currencies.

7. The float of SDRns would build as trading in the currency proved functional. Additionally, international trade would be expanding and swaps would increase in frequency. Consequently, the amount of convertible currency required from the Group of Ten and associates to meet foreign exchange requirements of the authorized banks would be much less than the nominal amounts loaned originally to the debtor nations.

It would be important to have the export credit agencies of countries in the Group of Ten and associates guarantee convertibility of payments in SDRns. This would build confidence in the system among suppliers and contractors. If the authorized banks refuse to exchange SDRns for other currencies or if they charge more than the established fee schedule for the transaction, the export credit agency would make the exchange in that country's currency.

The Terms of New and Converted Credits

The primary difference between Alternative 1 and the Chapter 6 solution are (1) the significantly higher amount of new credits made available in Alternative 1 to stimulate growth, and (2) the conversion of credits from private banks to soft SDRn loans is limited to those loans that are excessively expensive, chronically in arrears, or other special features. Components of the Chapter 6 solution could be used in most of the alternatives described in this chapter.

It is proposed that interest rates would be within the 3% to 6% range discussed in Chapter 6 and that the incentive system for debt service performance be included. The low rates are required to prevent the additions to total debt from making the interest-only debt service obligations oppressively high in the early stages of implementing the solution.

Grace periods should be no less than five years; ten would assure sustained expansion. Principal payment would be made over at least twenty years. This would make the average maturity about thirty years. Very long-term loans are a means whereby creditor countries accept some responsibility for the crisis. The discounting effect of inflation over this time period would substantially reduce the loan in real terms.

The Group of Ten guidelines mentioned above should secure the amount of foreign exchange dedicated to debt service. Each debtor nation would have a convertible currency cash flow schedule for ten years into the future. It would recast the standard balance of international payments statement by identifying (1) cash inflow according to projected foreign exchange earnings by source and new borrowings and (2) cash outflow that gives priority to interest and principal (if any) each year and accounts for imported goods and services, unrequited transfers, and other capital outflow. The priority given to interest and principal payments is a key feature. Another is an addendum that identifies applications of new borrowings. It would be updated each year to reflect current and revised future conditions.

Advantages and Disadvantages

The inflationary impact is minimal. Normal price pressures from expanded demand would occur, and cost-push factors would build as growth accelerates and capacity utilization exceeds 90%. However, the typical escalation based on a devaluation and the resultant sharp additions to money supply would be minimal. Use of SDRns would be limited to transactions between a sovereign state and lenders, supplier, or contractors, and between these latter organizations and authorized SDRn dealers.

The solution could be implemented quickly. Weeks instead of months would be required to define the concept in detail and to negotiate the terms with individual countries. Technocrats could operate with little political interference, using criteria conceived to discourage bickering and irregularities in terms between countries. Opposition to the solution could come from countries that have been taking strides to prevent a financial crisis. They could resist the cost of the SDRn concept and might want the United States to accept a disproportionate share of the backing for the new currency. The need for a solution and the hope for sustained recovery should lead to compromises.

A major disadvantage to the SDRn concept is that required growth to achieve foreign exchange generation adequate for both debt service and development is high. The 4% would be difficult to sustain, and many years of prosperity would be needed to strengthen economies. Allowing for recessions, peaks of 6% would be necessary. Success has a low probability.

Adding to foreign debt as a means of solving the

debt problem is a gamble. Many countries do not have the dynamic capabilities of Brazil and Korea. While some lessons have been learned, debtor nations will tend to repeat past mistakes. Therefore, the author believes that this solution will only postpone the time when a new financial crisis will occur and another solution will be required; however, at that stage the foreign debt levels would be crushingly high. It would be better to implement a solution that substantially reduces present external debt in real terms.

ALTERNATIVE 2: INTEREST RATE SUBSIDIES

The precedent for multiyear rescheduling has been established. Grace periods of five years have been granted Mexico, and a greater number of years would not be an obstacle. Most analysts do not expect recovery of principal for decades. Basically, technical default can be avoided if interest payments are kept current.

Many countries are restructuring their loan profile to reduce US$ content because of high interest rates and a strong U.S. dollar. However, even the lower rates in Europe, Japan, and other money markets are higher than most debtor nations can tolerate in a recession, and exchange rate risk will be a factor when there is movement out of the U.S. dollar (US$). Nevertheless, as 1986 begins, a large portion of the external debt will remain in U.S. dollars. Both the American prime rate and LIBOR will be rising from early 1985 levels (10.5% and 9.1%, respectively). At that time the total foreign debt will be so high that future interest payments will appear doubtful, especially if these rates have reached the 12% to 15% range.

Example of the Interest Rate Subsidy

Alternative 2 involves individual creditor governments paying the difference between (1) the cost of money and a bank administration fee (no profits would be permitted) and (2) very low interest rates. Specifically, Country X is currently paying an average of 12.5 % interest on principal, but it would pay only 3.5% under this solution. (The 3% to 6% range described in Chapter 6 with the associated incentive system should be applied in this alternative.) If total principal outstanding in US$25 billion, interest due would be US$3,125 million without the subsidy alternative.

When the solution is implemented, the payments received

by the banks holding the loan contracts would be US$875 million from the debtor nation and US$2,000 million from the government involved. Deletion of US$250 million from the subsidy would take place after crediting the administration fee and debiting the profit component of the interest rate. Summarizing, of the US$3,125 million originally due, the banks relinquish 8% (US$250 million), debtor Country X pays 38%, and the creditor government providing the subsidy pays 64% (US$2,000 million). In practice, individual loans that are composed of syndications involving banks from several countries would require prorations of individual loans. The overall responsibility of nations in which lenders are headquartered is a function of computing their composite share of total foreign debt.

Technical default does not occur because prompt interest payments can be made and, when principal is due in several years, the economy would be theoretically much stronger.

It is probable that governments would commit to only a limited time for the subsidies. Using the above example, the time period at the 64% level could be four years. An 8% reduction could then take place each year for eight years. Consequently, in the twelfth year the final 8% is paid. This could also coincide with the end of the grace period. Therefore, in this case the debtor nation will be paying full interest and principal at the end of the 1990s, but the amounts are much smaller percentages of GDP and foreign exchange earnings because of inflation.

Advantages and Disadvantages

The advantages of the solution are:

1. Administrative details are much less than the recommended solution. Loan contract charges are similar to the rescheduling procedures; therefore, it could be implemented quickly. Legal fees and other setup expenses would be much less.
2. Ongoing administration is handled by the banks. Operating expenses would be less than for establishing a new bureaucracy, especially if incentives were created for efficiencies.
3. Influence is gained over bank relationships with debtor nations. Complete compliance with all regulations and revised guidelines for lending procedures, including risk analysis and forecasting, could be better enforced.

The primary disadvantage is that the politicians and

voters in their constituencies would accept such a solution only under extreme conditions. The motivation is clearly to save the banking system. It could be sold to the public as a new Marshall Plan. The campaign to sell the solution could stress the need for a new era of prosperity and for some some acceptance of responsibility for the foreign debt problem. Criticism about paying a large percentage of interest due will focus on the bankers who were overly aggressive in marketing. In the case of the United States, the subsidies will certainly be related to the federal budget deficits and their impact on interest rates.

Another disadvantage is that governments paying the interest subsidy gain little leverage over the performance of the debtor nations. Performance standards and guidelines could be established as a basis for proceeding, but once the contract is signed, much depends on trust. Yet the debtor nation government may not wish to expedite payment from the direct borrower because of internal politics or other priorities for foreign exchange. To gain adherence to agreed upon economic and fiscal measures, the governments paying the subsidy would have to use the present approach involving the IMF.

One other disadvantage is that considerable time would be required to consolidate the number of borrowers into a small number of contracts involving only the government of the debtor nation; in the meantime, the subsidy could be paid on loans for questionable applications (for instance, blatant corruption could be involved).

Supplementary Issues

The debtor nation will not have adequate working capital to begin trading and economic development unless the Group of Ten agrees to provide concessionary loans through the IMF and World Bank, as suggested in Chapter 6.

Consolidation of the loan contracts into a few large loans owed directly by the debtor nation would be advisable. The private or parastatal borrower could pay the government in local currency. In addition to simplifying the administration, consolidation puts a buffer between the creditor governments paying subsidies and debtor nation loans that could involve blatant corruption, poorly conceived projects, and irregularities that could undermine support for the solution.

It would be better if all net creditor countries adopted the same approach and offered uniform terms to debtor nations. Awkward situations could arise if, for example, the United States were paying the subsidy for all debtor nations with loans from American banks and France selected only those with commercial potential. One step toward globally identical terms would be for the Group of Ten to design a system for the subsidy, and for such international organizations as the IMF, the World Bank, and other to adopt the terms.

ALTERNATIVE 3: LOAN WRITE-OFFS

The concept involves writing off a substantial part of the principal due to all foreign creditors. This write-off by the banks and other lenders decreases the amount on which interest is calculated and thereby lowers interest payments, regardless of the rate designated in the loan contract. Long grace periods and multiyear rescheduling would accompany the write-off. The concession from lenders would have economic and fiscal stipulations to assure improved performance on economic expansion as well as debt service.

Example of the Write-offs

This alternative solves the problem created by needing lower interest payments, but having a high cost of money. Spreads would reflect market conditions in the way that they do not at present. To accomplish the objective of reviving economic prosperity, the write-off would have to be 50% to 70%. Using the example in Alternative 2 (US$25 billion in total foreign debt, 12.5% average interest rate, US$3,125 million annual interest payment), a 60% write-off is agreed as the percentage needed to revive world prosperity. Foreign debt would be US$10 billion upon implementation of the solution. The interest payment per year would be US$1,250 million. This amount of interest based on US$25 billion represents a 5% rate and is within the 3% to 6% target range.

Many banks would fail if a 60% write-off took place. Without government intervention, confidence would plummet and a bank panic would start. Therefore, the write-off must be in conjunction with government issuance of special long-term bonds or notes for part of the write-off. A 50–50 split of the 60% would be reasonable, if the 30% undertaken by the banks does not cause excessive failures and added budget allocations to save depositors (the potential problem is mostly in the United States). The sacrifices demanded by the public for rescuing the banks would come from the 30% loss of assets and lower levels of interest earned.

In the example, net creditor countries issue long-term bonds for US$7.5 billion, each government assigning the appropriate amount to the banks within its responsibility. These lenders write off US$7.5 billion; in combination with the foreign loans still in effect, they have US$17.5 billion in assets, or 70% of the nominal value of the loans before the solution is implemented.

Advantages and Disadvantages

The primary advantage of the write-off solution is that nations with regulations that limited lending to Third World countries and created adequate reserves against bad loans will incur little impact from the solution. Countries that inadequately regulated the flow of loans to debtor nations and subsequently managed their reserve levels poorly will absorb the brunt of the write-offs. The United States will be the primary actor in implementing the solution.

The government's portion of the write-off is in the form of long-term bonds. The banking system of some countries is sufficiently strong to bypass the bond approach; only mergers of weaker banks would be necessary. If bonds are used, short-term goals are achieved with no immediate cash going directly to the banks. Budgets will have huge deficits in the United States, as described previously, but none of the solutions avoid this problem.

The primary disadvantage is the impact on the American banking system, already weakened by bad domestic loans. The recession will be causing defaults and foreclosures, and a 25% to 35% write-off of foreign loans would be a crushing blow to the solvency of many banks. Alternative 3 requires parallel programs for depositor protection on a large scale, as well as soft loans for banks that need liquidity and time to recover from the write-off decision.

The "principle of principal" is put aside. It is fundamental to have all parties understand that this exception is a one-time occurrence. Nevertheless, the resolve to honor international obligations could be permanently damaged. Such countries as Singapore and Switzerland may opt not to participate in the write-off program on this basis.

Supplementary Issues

This alternative would include the international organizations. Their capital base is dependent on the creditor countries and can be restored. In fact, the need for working capital by debtor nations to replenish inventories and refurbish the infrastructure described in Chapter 6 would necessitate major injections of funds at the time that a solution is implemented.

Short-term maturities would be written off at the selected rate (50% to 70% range), remaining short-term unless the lender negotiates conversion to medium-term maturities.

Trade credits would not be included. Payment arrangements would be stipulated in the contract covering the write-off. Arrears and accumulated interest would require special financing to create a fresh beginning. This could be part of the IMF and World Bank credits for the start-up phase. Exporters or government guarantee agencies must recover full invoice amounts. Otherwise, countries might delay payment and negotiate for an overall discount on amounts due. The solution must not encourage irregularities.

Miscellaneous points to considered include:

1. A system of incentives and penalties is needed to maintain debtor nation discipline. Prompt payments could narrow the spread and create access to concessionary loans. Penalties should involve more than late payment fees. Reversion of IMF and World Bank loans to commercial terms is a possibility, but others affecting recovery are feasible.

2. The details of stipulations other than loan terms must be explicit. Also, the additions to money supply, the goals for budget and current account deficits, trade credit arrangement, and similar categories should have the same incentive/penalty system as the one used for payments.

3. Banks needing cash to survive the write-offs and the transition to improved financial condition should be able to use the long-term bonds issued as the government's part in the write-off as collateral for loans from FDIC.

Alternative 3 is not an interim step that could be part of another solution. The write-off is permanent and gives a one-time opportunity to tie debtor nations to terms that are good for both parties, but that might be unpopular. A large loss of assets will be opposed by bankers not in danger of failing, but all viable solutions will involve a similar loss.

ALTERNATIVE 4: CONVERSION OF DEBT TO EQUITY

Instead of writing off 50% to 75% of the debt, the lenders accept ownership of assets in the debtor nation. Private borrowers in Mexico are currently proposing this option to their lenders. Malaysia is trying to privatize their economy. This is an indirect means of attracting foreign exchange to assist with debt service and to improve operating efficiency, which could increase exports.

Example of Debt to Equity

The scope of the debt has become immense relative to the size of most economies. As an example, using the debtor nation with US$25 billion in foreign obligation that is attempting to achieve a reduction in interest payments to US$1,250 million, US$15 billion would have to be converted to equity (assumes the 12.5% average interest rate used previously).

It is also necessary that the shares and property owned by the lender meet specifications of the bank examiners in the creditor countries. The original loans are assets that are to be repaid in convertible currency. This alternative proposes that assets valued in the local currency are adequate to offset depositor liabilities. Finding a buyer to recover a lender's capital at a future time would usually be difficult, and the price would be uncertain. Without question the nominal value of the assets would have to be discounted, probably by one-third. Many financial analysts would want a 50% discount. Using 50%, it would take US$30 billion of nominal assets to replace US$15 billion in loans.

A possibility would be to combine Alternative 3 with Alternative 4. One combination would be to write off 30%, convert 30% to equity, and retain 40% in foreign debt. The governments in which the lending banks are located need not become directly involved; however, if a guarantee on the resale value of the assets would be offered, the discount percentage could be decreased to 80% to 90% (each government would want some discount to assure recovery of principal).

In the combination alternative, if 40% remains in foreign debt, the country with US$25 billion would have US$10 billion based on the 12.5% average interest rate. The write-off portion would be US$7.5 billion. The remaining US$7.5 billion would be converted to ownership in the country's industries and properties; however, it would take US$11.25 billion in local assets to accomplish the conversion if bank examiners apply the one-third discount rule (the actual percentage would be in the 25% to 50% range). An 80% guarantee would reduce the needed local assets to US$9,375 billion.

Advantages and Disadvantages

Alternative 4 raises the issue of sovereignty. The politicians and technocrats in the debtor nations would be highly criticized for "giving away the country." The confiscatory aspects of a defaulting debtor would turn many against the capitalistic system. The political spectrum from right to center-left would probably lose large portions of their constituencies.

The discount factor would enrage the population still further. Very large portions of the economy would be deeded to foreigners because the foreign debt had grown even during the period of austerity in most cases. When 25% to 50% is added to the total to allow for potential loss of assets, an emotional reaction is almost certain. The operating environment for owners of the assets would be difficult. When redundancies are eliminated and labor saving mechanization is introduced, organized labor would be revitalized.

At the beginning, implementation of the debt to equity alternative could appear to be a giant bonanza. Then resistance to the "financial coup d'etat" would build, and the newly acquired assets would appear to be a severe liability. However, with effective public relations, economic expansion, job training and formation, and resource development, private enterprise could make the new operations profitable. Most of the new businesses would be highly risky, and earnings would have to be significantly higher than corporate standards to justify buying assets from the banks.

The primary advantage for net creditor countries is that the sacrifice is made almost wholly by the debtor nations, if there is no write-off of loans by the banks. Therefore, the combination of debt to equity and write-offs is required for a balanced solution. Otherwise, the banks would have the potential of a capital gain, selling at a profit or at a net discount that is less than that required by the bank examiners to protect depositors. The countries in which the banks are located have no cash outflow; a few banking systems, particularly in the United States, will need intervention, as mentioned.

Supplementary Issues

The 30% write-off in the combination alternative means that many banks will require rescuing, as previously mentioned. Soft loans, conversion of debt to equity, and mergers will involve government intervention. The failure rate will be high because both bad domestic and foreign loans will be in trouble.

International organizations would be writing off 30% of their assets in loans and would need funds for new loans to debtor nations. Therefore, Group of Ten members would have sizeable assessments.

Procedures for any form of conversion of debt to equity would include the following steps:

1. The debtor nation identifies the assets offered. Examples include state-owned utilities, petroleum companies, transportation operations, and manufacturing and mining operations. Property for tourism development, natural resource exploitation, and commercial and industrial expansion would be included. Deception, inflation of estimated values, and legal traps must be expected.

2. The banks appraise the assets. Prospective buyers of the bank's new operating companies and properties and other respected experts would make up the assessment team for such appraisal.

3. It is probable that the banks would request more assets because (a) many appraisals would be less than the country's estimate, (b) some assets would be unacceptable, and (c) attractive investments not on the original list would be identified by the teams of appraisers. Some nationalizations might be necessary at this stage in order to provide the required value of assets. The prior owners would be compensated in the local currency.

4. Negotiations to reach an agreeable price would begin. Incentive to reach agreements on the individual assets quickly would come from having interest due on the full amount (US$25 billion in the example) until the complete package is ready for signing. The process would be time-consuming. Emotions would reach extremes. Some countries might withdraw from the negotiations because the cost in foreign ownership would be too high. Strong feelings would be exchanged about demands for majority control, complete decision-making authority, and personnel reductions to improve profits.

5. Appraisals on the added assets would be included in the negotiations as the teams return and the formal reports are completed. The second, third, and fourth phase (more than two are probable) of negotiations would involve painful negotiations to reach the required amount of assets. Economies would be in poor condition, and interest would be accumulating.

It is probable that Alternative 4 would not survive the five steps, and considerable time and money would have been wasted.

ALTERNATIVE 5: SHARP DEVALUATION OF THE U.S. DOLLAR (US$)

The solution requires the Reagan administration to accelerate the decline of the U.S. dollar (US$) during 1986. A return to Autumn 1978 rates would not be adequate to reduce the foreign debt burden of most countries significantly. Parity with the Swiss franc would probably be enough; this implies rates of US$1 = ¥100 and DM1.25. The decline expected by the end of 1986 without deliberate devaluation would be US$1 = Sfr2.00, ¥200, and DM2.50.

Example of the US$ Devaluation Concept

The objective of this alternative is to reduce a country's foreign debt in US$s relative to other currencies. Obligations in US$s become much less expensive and export earnings in this currency are greatly increased. For example, a Brazilian-made blouse is sold for DM20; this is worth US$5.70 in early 1985, but with this solution by end-1986, US$16.00 are earned from the transaction. No default on debt service occurs because the obligation has been reduced 64%.

The devaluation theory has major limitation in actual practice. First, it is difficult to visualize the Reagan administration agreeing to anything that diminishes the image of the United States or jeopardizes security (one result would be that military personnel stationed abroad would be in desperate personal financial condition). Second, devaluation in foreign exchange markets would take the following steps:

1. Deficit spending continues. The 1986–87 recession increases the budget deficit's percentage of GNP. As predicted, funding a major portion of the shortfall from abroad becomes impossible because of need for capital elsewhere and some loss of confidence in the U.S. dollar (US$).
2. Monetary policy changes, partly to fund the deficit and partly to stimulate the economy. Paul Volker resigns and is replaced by an advocate of the theory. Money supply increases sharply. Inflation reflects increased

liquidity and the higher costs of imports, and price escalation paces the rise in interest rates (private demand for money would be decreasing, but the government would be funding huge deficits).

3. Stagflation would ensue (negative growth and 15% to 18% inflation). Unemployment would rise above 12% in the trough of the recession, probably late 1987. However, because the US$ is highly devalued at that time, American products would be extremely competitive abroad. Recovery would begin in advanced technologies, highly modernized industries, and agricultural exports. Subsequently, a broad-based period of prosperity would develop.

The Reagan administration would apply monetary restraint once the recovery is established to return price escalation to a level below 10%. The government would be hampered by huge budget deficits requiring tax increases.

Advantages and Disadvantages

The success of Alternative 5 would be limited by the rise in American interest rates. The American prime rate would be at least 20%. Brazil would have to pay US$23 billion in interest. Mexico, confronted with falling crude oil prices, would owe US$20 billion, nearly twice their earning from petroleum exports. Technical default would occur quickly because foreign exchange generation would be inadequate to honor interest obligations.

In addition to the fatal impact of interest rates, export volume of debtor nations would be contracting because many countries had become dependent on U.S. imports, and the falling US$ would mean that American buyers could no longer afford foreign goods and services. The combination of sharply higher interest rates and contracting foreign exchange earnings would more than offset the gain from a devalued U.S. dollar.

Alternative 5 would certainly add to the problem rather than solve it. Advanced nations and Third World countries would lose a major market. American capital investment and tourism would be nil. International trade would be adversely affected by a depreciating US$. Defaults on debt service would multiply before the theoretical advantage of a weak US$ could be gained.

OVERVIEW

It is necessary to reduce the amount of interest paid each year by debtor nations to avoid technical default, political instability, and sustained economic recession. This can only be done by (1) substantially decreasing the rate, (2) substantially decreasing the principal amount on which the rate is calculated, (3) systematically capitalizing a large percentage of interest due and adding to principal outstanding, or (4) helping the debtor nation pay through a form of grant or subsidy.

Alternatively, net creditor countries can (1) significantly increase the foreign exchange earnings of the debtor nation through expanded trade so that debt service is not a problem or (2) reduce the interest and principal in real terms by devaluing the currency denominated in the loan contracts.

Each of the six methods to achieve the primary objectives stated at the beginning of the chapter have associated problems. Briefly stated by method, they are:

1. The cost of money is at least double the interest rate needed by most nations to maintain debt service and to emerge from depressed economic conditions. This means that privately owned banks would become financially troubled and would be highly criticized by shareholders for extending much lower rates to, for example, the Philippines than to IBM. Logic dictates that these banks must be replaced by net creditor governments that offer artificially low fixed rates. The complexities of this process are explained in Chapter 6, but the reductions are feasible.

2. The principle of principal is lost if the foreign debt is written off totally or substantially. Lessons learned in the 1982–85 period have not all been constructive. Major debtors now know that they have power to influence terms for rescheduled debt because banks become desperate to avoid technical default. Some governments have entered into agreements with no intention of honoring the terms. The key issue is that financial integrity has declined. Writing off most of the outstanding debt will further weaken the resolve to pay.

3. Capitalizing unpaid interest, directly or indirectly, is not a solution. It is the approach that the IMF and the Americans have been using since September 1982 when Mexico needed rescuing. The total debt increases, and the maintenance and expansion of the industrial infrastructure required to service the added debt does not take place. Cuts in government spending, import controls, tight money, and reduced external demand weaken the operating condition of productive facilities. The 1983–85 period of prosperity in advanced countries has disguised the deterioration that has taken place in debtor nations.

4. Grants and subsidies are acceptable applications of public funds when the recipient if poverty stricken or strategically critical. The banks, which have earned huge sums in interest and fees from Third World countries, do not qualify for either category. A third justification is to correct a wrongdoing, and the government offering the grant or subsidy to the debtor nation could rationalize this use of taxpayer funds by acknowledging that its policies and regulations permitted excess. The actual recipients are the banks, however. And this will be difficult to justify with high unemployment in a recession. Even preventing loss of depositor savings by giving money to the banks would be difficult to sell to the public when people are homeless and starving. It is ironic that this solution is the simple, fastest way for net creditor countries to handle the crisis and that grants and subsidies would be the cheapest approach for the United States. A very low probability exists that the solution in any form will be implemented.

5. The time for significantly increasing the foreign exchange earnings of debtor nations was two years ago during the expansion phase of the present business cycle. The funds needed to generate internal real growth as well as increased external trade would have been an enormous addition to foreign debt, and the exports would have added to the American trade deficit. Regardless, 1983–84 was the period during which the SDRn solution could have been attempted. It probably would have failed and would have worsened the crisis that is imminent. Clearly, attempting such a solution in the contraction phase is unwise.

6. Devaluation of the U.S. dollar (US$) must be dismissed as a solution. Interest rates that would result from budget deficits, inflation, and tight money policies would cause default on interest payments before the debtor nations could benefit from a much cheaper U.S. dollar.

Important Factors in the Solution's Design

The American banking system is in fragile condition (1985) because of deregulation, loans to foreign countries, an agricultural financial crisis partly caused by the strong US$, and a large number of bad domestic loans. Solutions dealing with the foreign loans must consider the implication for U.S. banks that are in trouble and have no exposure abroad. For example, write-off or subsidies could not be offered to debtor nations without offering similar programs to financially stricken farmers. Many American banks will fail in the next recession, and the government will find that answers to all four causes will be required.

Another major complication is the range of vulnerability to the financial crisis among net creditor countries. The Group of Ten and other financially strong countries is arrayed between Switzerland (100% bad debt reserves, low foreign loan exposure) and the United States (low bad debt reserves, high foreign loan exposure). Specific solutions must deal with this range, and yet allow the United States sufficient latitude to stabilize the U.S. dollar (US$) at reasonable exchange rates and to have a viable banking system capable of supporting international trade. The approach taken in this book is to retain the rights of sovereign decision making within a net creditor country and also to have common policies and terms when these governments are dealing with debtor nations.

The third factor is the possibility of the BIS or IMF playing a greater role in the alternative solutions. At present, the IMF is identified with adjustment (austerity) programs that have alienated many debtor nations. It is, therefore, recommended that the preliminary design originate with an ad hoc committee of the Group of Ten. When the optimal solution is ready for discussion, the probability for success in the subsequent four phases could be increased by the BIS and/or IMF (1) acting as intermediaries to resolve differences in the process of achieving a final solution design, (2) providing administrative services in the organization phase before implementing the solution, (3) collecting and distributing debt service payments, (4) monitoring payments, sociopolitical and economic performance, and government policies for loan contract infractions, and (5) offering centralized accounting control.

In addition, certain components of the negotiations could be best handled by such informed third parties as the BIS and IMF. Moreover, aspects of the solution could utilize these respected organizations to achieve goals quickly. Time is important, and all resources should be considered in averting the crisis.

REFERENCES

A Survey of Central Banking. *The Economist,* 22 September 1984.

Cerami, Charles A. We Need a Marshall Plan for the 80's. *The New York Times,* 20 January 1985.

de Larosiere, J. *External Debt in Perspective.* International Monetary Fund, September 1983.

Erdman, Paul. Living on the Default Line. *Playboy,*

October 1983.

Kenen, Peter B. A Bailout Plan for the Banks. *The New York Times,* 6 March 1983.

The International Debt Crisis. Swiss Ad Hoc Group on International Debt Problems, August 1984.

8

Defending Against the Financial Crisis— Banks and Companies

It is fundamental to consider what will optimize profit performance in the period of prosperity that will follow implementing one of the solutions discussed in Chapters 6 and 7. However, banks and companies that do not implement defensive measures during 1985–86 in preparation for severe recession in 1987 may find themselves more concerned about survival in the late 1980s than about optimizing earnings in the 1990s.

COUNTRY WINNERS AND LOSERS

Some countries, freed from crushing foreign debt service, have the human and natural resources to generate strong economic growth at end-decade and into the 1990s. They will have learned from mistakes in the 1970s and 1980s. More economic and financial mistakes will, of course, be made. Sociopolitical developments will prevent them from realizing full potential. Yet, these countries—both advanced and developing—will offer decades of efficient operations and convertible currency profits. France and Korea are examples of long-term winners.

Causes of a country being a long-term loser vary. Chronic sociopolitical instability could stem from (1) population growth resulting in over 40% of the people being under 20 years old and having a low probability of ever working consistently, (2) a corrupt leadership that has siphoned capital from planned fixed assets, training of human resources, and social development into personal wealth accumulation, or (3) the many other causes associated with ethnic groups, ideology, language, racism, and religion. Most of the leaders could be incompetent. The country might not have exportable resources. A basic work ethic could be lacking. Regardless of specific causes, Nigeria, the Philippines, and Venezuela are examples of long-term losers for most banks and companies.

Aspects to consider about a country's potential are listed below.

1. Problem solving, resource development, and other factors will create opportunities within a country that have sufficient priority to warrant foreign exchange for goods and services, remittance of profits, payment of royalties, and other transactions. Therefore, a loser for the majority might be a winner in certain instances.

2. Some countries with large populations have important natural resources, or a portion of the work force with highly qualified people, or long-term consumer market potential for specific products, or some other factor that is attractive to foreign business. Unfortunately, these countries also have characteristics associated with losers. Banks and companies will find that many of these countries cannot be ignored in the strategic planning process. Brazil, India, and Indonesia are examples of places where specific opportunities will arise.

3. Countries that are heavily dependent on exports of nonfood commodities are likely to be long-term losers. Most minerals will recover modestly from low prices in the 1986–88 period. Countries that add plants to process the commodities could escape the loser category, but these sources of foreign exchange are subject to substitution by wholly new concepts and synthetic materials. Capital intensive extractive operations in high-risk countries rarely meet company standards for return on investment. Consequently, private firms are assisting governments to establish and manage locally owned operations because of their need for exports, job formation, and real economic growth. Consequently, shortages of nonfood commodities are unlikely; and Chile, Peru, Zaire, and others are in fundamental trouble.

4. Clear winners will have human resources who can optimize information processing and create or utilize advanced technology. The evolution from industrial complexes that employ large numbers of people with limited skills to smaller plants that need highly trained personnel is creating

structural social change. Countries with people having heterogeneous cultural backgrounds, particularly the United States, will evolve toward two distinctly different populations living in the same space. One is a technocratic elite and those who assist their work. The other is an underclass composed of people with lower-level service jobs, the unemployed, organized crime groups, exploited illegal aliens, and youth trapped in ghettos. Security precautions will become paramount in these cases, whereas in Japan and Sweden the issues will be different.

STRATEGIC PLANNING—THE STEPS TO TAKE

Banks and companies (B/C) have to become highly selective in the deployment of resources in international business. Figure 8–1 summarizes the identification of country winners and losers for the organization. This assessment is the first step and should be made independently of where the B/C currently has operations of any type.

Figure 8–1. Winners and Losers for the Individual Bank or Company

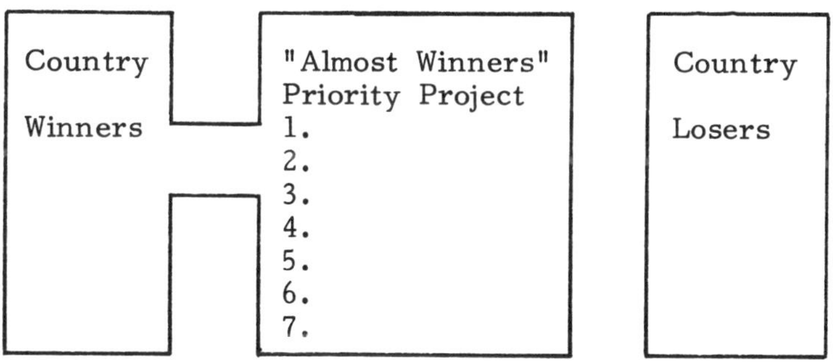

The second step is to place the B/C's existing businesses abroad in a cell of the matrix shown in Figure 8–2. Place only the winners in the cells. List operations in loser countries. Also list "almost winners"; these are the places of secondary priority. If the B/C can profitably confine its future business abroad to the winners, consideration of "almost winners" will not be necessary.

The third step is to establish rate of return (ROR) standards for each cell. These standards weigh country risk, critical importance to overall profits, and such factors as contractual commitments and management aggressiveness.

Figure 8–2. Country Winners Matrix

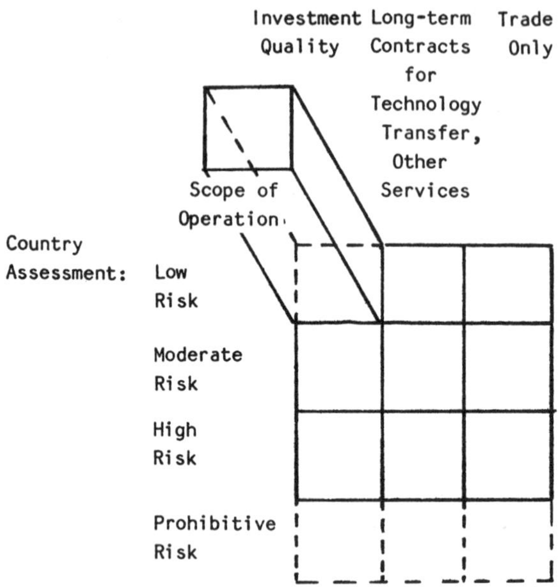

Tolerance of risk varies widely among executives, and each B/C will have an individualistic approach to setting standards. Consequently, every operation within a country winner could have a different ROR, and the average for countries could vary widely. The important point is that standards are established as a basis for strategic decision making.

After the first three steps, a B/C can identify operations presently above, below, and approximately equal to expected profitability in country winners. The fourth step involves analysis of why there are departures from the ROR. This involves an evaluation of personnel, regulatory framework, government interrelationships, facilities, and the many factors related to individual businesses. The economy of some countries could be out of phase with the global business cycle.

The fifth step is to prepare a forecast of future profitability. It is based on no major changes in the composition and scope of operations. It looks realistically at the 1986–88 period and determines the condition of the business at the depth of the trough. In 1985–86 this is a short-range forecast. A longer-range view of possibilities in the early 1990s (five-year forecast) is also needed to estimate resiliency in the recovery phase. Some assumptions must be made about factors that are external to the operation, as well as about the internal situation involving management, low-cost improvements, and other changes that could be made within the expected budget.

The five steps complete a corporate self-analysis. An estimation of "what" and "why" has been completed for each business abroad in three time periods: present, trough condition, and five-year outlook.

Constructing a Plan of Action

A basic approach to sorting what needs to be done and the order in which the actions are to be taken involves a decision-tree. Invest, divest, or hold are the initial three branches. Within each are alternative possibilities. Two primary objectives control all decisions: (1) the parent B/C must control losses and prevent operations during 1986–88 from threatening its financial stability, and (2) the B/C must be prepared to seize the special opportunities that will develop in the crisis by having a strategic plan with priorities.

The subbranches of the investment branch are (1) operate at existing facilities with minimal cash injections, (2) expand market share in present product lines by investing in plant, equipment, and working capital at existing locations, and (3) expand product lines and market shares during the crisis by acquiring facilities from distressed B/Cs. The executive using the decision-tree assigns a probability to each subbranch based on information developed in the five steps taken for each business in a country winner. The total cannot exceed 1.0 or 100% (for example, 0.5, 0.3, and 0.2, or 50%, 30%, and 20%).

The cautious manager may not be convinced that debt service will be substantially less later in the 1980s. Conditions may not justify a withdrawal, but his forecast indicates that fresh capital committed to the venture should be kept at the lowest possible level. Rationalization of all business activities should take place. The primary goal is to achieve the lowest possible unit costs without major commitments of capital. A later return to profitable operations would then be judged on an investment level that has been controlled.

A more optimistic manager would launch an aggressive marketing campaign with accompanying product modifications to increase market share. The goal is to have a larger percentage of total sales in the market when demand rises and thus to have more revenue to cover fixed costs. In combination with the economies achieved during the years of low demand, the venture is in the optimal position to earn a high level of profits in the future. Management must take the bold step of allocating significant amounts of capital to a venture that is currently losing money.

The third subbranch involves an even more aggressive strategy for the 1980s. It recognizes that some B/Cs will come close to financial collapse and will require rescuing. This daring approach can be solely an extension of the second subbranch. Additions to market share are accomplished by acquiring competing operations. Or acquisitions at very attractive prices in new product lines with potential when demand surges can be included to permit both expansion and diversification. The goal is to greatly strengthen the operation as opportunities arise during the troubled years.

Disposition of Ventures in Country Losers

Selling all or a portion of the operation is not accomplished easily because the B/C will want convertible currency for its assets, directly or through an acceptable barter arrangement. In addition, the government is likely to be concerned about losing access to advanced technology. Nevertheless, considering divestment as the main branch, the potential buyers become the subbranches in this case. They are (1) the government, (2) private nationals with access to convertible currency (sub-subbranches are direct government support, such indirect government support as approval for a barter transaction or use of export earnings, and capital deposited abroad), and (3) foreign investors (sub-subbranches are B/Cs with existing operations in the country or B/Cs predicting recovery and looking for a means of entry).

The government might acquire the assets if nonmoney concerns are resolved and if the package did not aggravate a current convertible currency crisis. Creativeness is needed to structure the payment schedule, utilize barter alternatives, and provide solutions to sources of management, technology, and any protected processes, patents, and trademarks. Timing may be important. A wave of nationalism might offer an opportunity to sell out or reduce percentage ownership. Retaining a small minority that could be written off is a tactic to be considered because of the assurances it gives nationals in nonmoney aspects and because of the access to information that might be helpful in conflicts about payment performance on shares sold.

Private nationals are possibilities if they are sufficiently influential to obtain government support or have funds abroad that can be used for the transaction. In a few cases, locally owned companies have international operations that generate profits that can be legally used for the acquisition. Normally, if conditions are so bad in a country that divestment is being considered, it is unlikely that anything other than a barter arrangement is possible. A portion of the output is often the basis of payment, or a three-way relationship is possible in which the buyer of the shares purchases a specified material or product in the local currency and ships the goods to the seller as payment.

Caution about notes promising future payment in convertible currency is necessary because of (1) long-term foreign exchange shortages, (2) a possible change in government and abrogation of the contract, (3) bankruptcy of the operation under local management, and (4) simple refusal to pay. Tying withdrawal to a technical assistance contract and creating dependency of the new owners on the B/C's expertise is one means of assuring adherence to the contract. Another means is providing export markets through the seller.

Foreign investors may be optimistic and want to buy. They may have a forecast that indicates a surge in demand as previously mentioned and a long-term strategy in which the country plays a vital role. Or a buyer may have accumulated currency in a country winner from the viewpoint of the seller (an exception, therefore, to the "only convertible currency" rule), and a form of swap is negotiated. A match is needed. A government with B/Cs in troubled countries could play the role of intermediary.

The three subbranches of divestment are given a probability in the same way that they were assigned to investment alternatives. These probabilities sent priorities in the allocation of time and resources in developing a buyer.

Disposition of Unsold Assets

When no buyer can be found, the business must either operate with minimum input of fresh capital or be "mothballed." The latter option has only one advantage. An asset can be made ready for production when conditions improve, and the benefits derived from the sale of a going concern can be realized with minimal drain on capital during the 1986–88 period. However, it also costs money to mothball office and plant and to reassign or terminate personnel.

Adding to unemployment would anger the host government, and officials would want strict adherence to worker rights at the time of plant closure. A carefully planned phase-out using attrition, elimination of some product lines, and a communications campaign with the government, unions, and employees might reduce some of the cost. In a few cases the operation to be sold is earning profits in the local currency, and the pressure to mothball is nil. However, if the facility cannot be sold and the plant is losing large sums of money, the decision maker has no option.

The mothballing subbranches are immediate shutdown and "walk away" (doubtful right to return), controlled shutdown with negotiated exit and delineated right to return, and a phase-out plan based on a cost/benefit analysis of the time and money involved. Some B/Cs have given the assets to the employees as a form of "walk away." In other cases, premature disclosure of plans caused emotions to be high, and expatriates were instructed to leave on short notice. A prolonged phase-out has the possible disadvantage of appearing to plot against the government, unions, and employees. The objectives of creating goodwill for a possible return and reducing the net costs of mothballing could be reversed.

The B/C has a wide range of options if a country loser is involved and returning is not part of the long-term plan. However, honorable behavior is advisable because actions will be known in other countries. Careful attention to details on tactics, timing, and decisions affecting personnel is necessary. A sub-subbranch of both "walk away" and phase-out is early disclosure of plans and what to do.

Figure 8–3 summarizes the decision-tree dealing with the strategy for country winners and losers in the 1980s. Each business situation will differ. Even in the same country, specific conditions will change the probabilities assigned by two different banks or two different companies with similar operations.

It is important to realize that the probability of a perfect course of action is low. The final probability is calculated by first considering the three branches, then the subbranches, and then the sub-subbranches that are placed on the tree. The purpose of the technique is to improve the possibility of selecting the optimal course of action by knowing all the alternatives and by systematically identifying the likelihood of each alternative occurring. The quality of judgment being used in the decision-making process is the most important element, but the end result will be assisted by use of decision-tree.

Figure 8–3. Decision-tree for Strategic Planning in the 1980s

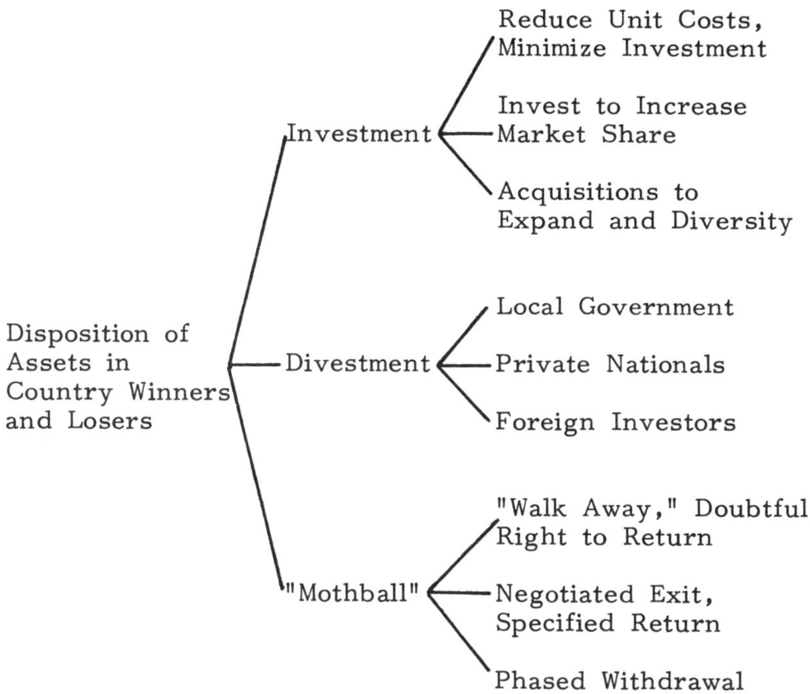

WORST CASE ANALYSIS

Successful business people have always asked the question, "What will be the results if the forecasts fall short of expectations?" Prudent executives have taken the time to determine whether there are reasonable chances that important factors will not turn out as predicted by supporters of a business proposal. "Worst case" does not necessarily deal with the doom and gloom extreme. Instead, it considers such possibilities as slower penetration of the market than stated in the sales forecast, a large capital cost overrun on a project, or an effective countertactic by a competitor.

Bankers have been particularly concerned about examining these contingencies when loans are going to private parties. Many seem to have placed this type of prudence to one side when extending credit to sovereign borrowers. The 1985–86 period is an important time to identify success factors in any business and examine what could go wrong.

Forecasting accuracy depends more on the qualifications of who is doing the predicting than on the sophistication of a quantitative method. Does that person have a newly received graduate degree? Is it the eternal optimist in marketing? Or is it the annoying pessimist in the controller's office? Access to relevant data is important, and quantitative forecasting methods are sometimes helpful. But many business situations cannot be translated into numbers. Moreover, times-series projections, multiple regressions, and other standard statistical techniques are apt to be misleading at a time when separate causes of major change are converging.

Judgment is the critical ingredient in a forecast. Too often, major decisions are made on the basis of predictions prepared by people who do not have the necessary operating and technical experience to inject the required judgment. Forecasts of sociopolitical conditions and other environmental factors are frequently prepared by personnel with little background in the appropriate field. Therefore, it is rational for managers to be cautious about accepting forecasts at face value.

The benefits of worst case analysis include the following:

1. Points are raised that modify parts of a project or proposal without killing it. The process of looking at the situation from a different perspective often identifies factors not previously considered. Overlooked regulations, understated costs, omitted markets, and other possibilities are corrected. In this case the probability of success is improved because needed refinements have been added.

2. The full extent of losses that might occur if actual results vary significantly from those in the proposal is estimated. It sometimes happens that these loses are so great that management opts not to go ahead. For example, the attractive interest and fees from a loan might be repaid. The analysis revealed a magnitude of loss that could not justify a "go" decision.

3. Contingency financing and responses to other possible developments can be prepared in advance of their happening. Instead of making decisions in a crisis atmosphere after the proposal proceeds, critical elements that might need strengthening are identified and standby solutions prepared.

4. Nonoperating factors, including sociopolitical condi-

tions, are frequently forced into the evaluation by worst case analysis. Such extracountry factors as adversity in neighboring countries can be pivotal in evaluating international loans and ventures. People with the appropriate experience understand the cultures involved and are able to foresee issues that require changes in terms and components.

5. The knowledge that a worst case analysis will be undertaken reduces the number of occasions when personnel exaggerate the benefits of a project or proposal. This is especially true if the analysis is regularly completed by employees or others who have no vested interest and who have adequate training and experience to judge the forecasts for critical factors.

The concept of worst case analysis should be a formal part of the decision-making process in a B/C. It can also be part of a manager's method of dealing with day-to-day responsibilities. Instead of automatically going ahead with the business situation because of the facts and forecasts presented, he considers the implications of what would occur if these forecasts did not happen as stated. Business needs ideas, positive thinking, and confidence that approved ventures will generate earnings, not losses. The critical point for B/Cs is that approval follows consideration of less optimistic possibilities.

SOME CONSIDERATIONS FOR MANAGEMENT FUNCTIONS

Managers of accounting, finance, marketing, operations, and personnel have specific steps to take in preparing for a potentially severe business downturn. The basic factors are discussed below. In addition, individual B/Cs will have specific complications that must be considered.

An important aspect of management thinking is to see beyond the doom and gloom. Nearly every defensive measure taken to reduce costs, debt service, inventories, and so on, should have an offensive counterpart that permits the B/C to seize opportunities and to move rapidly when the expansion phase of the business cycle begins.

Accounting

The average number of days for receivables lengthens in a recession. The controller should:

1. Know the impact on working capital and inform finance of the potential need for bank loans, identifying the

cash levels according to degree of recession severity, and relating these levels to objectives for cost cutting.

2. Coordinate with marketing to establish policies for collection methods by customer category. It is important that aggressive tactics to improve the flow of receivables do not alienate customers in a soft market.

A plan should be prepared for payables. It is possible to lower the cost of loans to bolster working capital by lengthening time over which invoices are paid. This is a delicate balance between supplier relationships, credit rating, and cash inflows. It is simplistic to apply a rule that the stretch being incurred on receivables should be applied equally to payables. The plan should be more selective, specifying categories such as A (prompt defined as xx days) to D (slow defined as xx days). In cases where the supplier is a customer, direct contact to resolve problems could be established as a policy.

Departments of administration and accounting should be the model for cost cutting. This means personnel reductions, mechanization of processing, and trimming of benefits and services. In conjunction with legal counsel, this organizational component must also conceive of ways for the whole of a B/C to (1) reduce salary levels despite union contracts, (2) eliminate the cost of expensive executives through early retirement schemes, phaseout dismissal programs (permits a person over 55 to have extra time to find employment), and consolidation of responsibilities, and (3) minimize the current financial burden of retirement program obligations.

In many cases, it will be the controller or head of administration that sees only the present situation and makes no allowance for the recovery phase of the business cycle. If the cutbacks are managed badly and the loyalty of personnel remaining with the B/C is lost, profitability after 1987 will be jeopardized. Top management must be certain that defensive measures are implemented, but also that a program of communications with retained employees makes them feel secure, confident, and aware of the "whys," "whens," and "wherefore" of the situation.

Finance

Money management is sometimes in administration and accounting, as well as finance. Regardless of location, the key issue is the overvalued U.S. dollar and the high probability that it will fall precipitously during 1986–87. Concern about forward cover in the U.S. dollar has played a role in supporting the extraordinary exchange rates that prevailed in early 1985. Conservative defensive positions in undervalued but potentially strong currencies will be prudent. The initial step to reduce foreign exchange losses is to establish strict policies for hedging during the next three years (through 1988).

Restructuring of the B/Cs debt position is probably necessary. Short-term maturities that cannot be repaid without new borrowing should be converted to medium-term loans with principal repayment after 1988 (or designed to have low installments in the early years and that increase in amount during the 1990s).

Any peaking of debt service obligations during 1986–88 should be refinanced. Caution about both exchange risk and interest rates is advised. Obligations in yen, Deutsche marks, Swiss francs, and a few other currencies usually requiring relatively low interest rates will be strengthening relative to the U.S. dollar, but the yen will also be gaining on the other strong currencies. Real interest rates will be less of a factor than safety and stability. The American inflation rate will rise sharply, interest rates will be high, although the exchange risk is minimal.

Finance should have arranged contingency financing by mid-1986. Standby credits is usually a standard function of the department. However, B/C income will be declining more rapidly than in previous recessions, and many normal sources of credit will be in serious trouble. These banks will not be realistic sources of new loans. Therefore, financial executives must decide who to borrow from and what currencies to target for the new loans. Foreign relationships established in restructuring the debt profile will be important.

Top management should be fully informed about major money management and borrowing decisions in the coming years. What is gained in internal economies can be lost by an amateur in international finance. In fact, solvency of the B/C could be at stake.

Marketing

The coordination with accounting on receivables has been mentioned. However, the head of marketing will concentrate on maximizing cash inflow. The key issues are (1) sales volume, (2) net prices after discounts, commission incentives, and special bonuses, and (3) such added expenses to maintain market share as increased advertising. Parallel to these points is marketing's contribution to cost reduction.

A marketing strategy should be devised that secures key accounts from competitors, targets financially strong customers, and considers the economic strength of some countries. High performance sales personnel should be matched with priority customers; this must consider established purchasing agent/sales person relationships, but a realignment of account assignments will normally be productive. Direct involvement of executive management could be part of the strategy.

The need to offer discounts, added commissions to agents, and similar steps to make sales will depend on the intensity of competition for a particular B/C in a contracting market. Technologically advanced products are less susceptible than traditional goods. The management of pricing in a deepening recession will be critical because of increased price elasticity.

Another important factor will be the marketing budget. Selective spending cuts are to be expected, but the direct selling effort should be supported to the extent possible. Sacrifices will be required. Any major budget reduction means losses of valuable information, multiple responsibilities by personnel being retained, and extra care in spending for services and supplies. The process of establishing priorities, looking for items to trim from the budget, and reviewing the performance of employees is beneficial to overall performance. Routines and traditional approaches are changed, and the B/C is better able to react quickly to worsening or improving conditions.

Operations

Planning to achieve optimal use of facilities and personnel when volume is decreasing and union pressure to maintain employment is increasing is pivotal to profit performance (or loss control). Using overtime instead of second shifts, selection of the most efficient equipment in closing down parts of a plant, and similar alternatives should be determined in advance of the recession. Computer simulation is a superior method of identifying the successive steps to take; the variables can be better controlled than in other business applications. Furthermore, the results can be a means of communicating costs and benefits to shop stewards and other union leaders.

Inventory control of product inputs, parts and supplies, and finished products is critical. As working capital becomes a problem, money committed to inventory becomes critical. It is imperative to achieve reductions at a pace consistent with a slower rate of sales. In addition, the purchasing agent for the B/C can ask the supplier to retain a greater inventory responsibility in return for a certain buying volume/price relationship. Safety stocks should be at minimum levels, using alternative sources of supply to avoid stockouts. Careful use of computerized information on lead times for orders will assist in lowering the safety level. However, very low inventory levels are dangerous in some countries because supplier plants may be located abroad, and the time between the order and unloading on the receiving dock is not consistent. In this case, judgment is necessary, and the basis of the decision should be recorded.

Two other factors should be considered. First, spending on maintenance should increase because it is important to keep those facilities selected in the plan operative. Second, tighter standards on benefits from capital items should be implemented. The two factors are related because less spending on new equipment means that the old equipment must keep running. In countries troubled by foreign exchange shortages, the need for maintenance and cannibalizing idle production lines is basic to survival because of import controls.

Personnel

Coordination of personnel reductions should take place through this department. Expertise about government regulations and union contracts in the process of discharging people is housed in personnel. The manager should have a plan for early reductions through attrition and subsequent terminations resulting from office and plant closures. Some jobs need replacements, and they should be known by personnel and the department involved.

Successful contraction of operations often depends on systematically reassigning responsibilities. Operations, marketing, and the other departments should be asked by personnel to create such a plan. For example, marketing would determine, for instance, if the manager of advertising is limited to eight people instead of ten, how the work would get completed and what sacrifice would there be in time.

Sometimes personnel will work with top management to redesign the B/C's organization when business is contracting. The divisions are consolidated. Subsidiaries in related products and services have the same general manager. Staff departments are taken from operating divisions and centralized at headquarters. These economies can be significant in cost control. They can also paralyze a B/C when the recovery begins. The design might be optimal for the lower level of business activity in a recession, but highly restrictive in an expansion phase.

Moderation in changes and reductions is prudent unless the B/C is in basic trouble. The best employees are also the most mobile employees. Heavy handed firing and overloading of remaining personnel will quickly drive the most competent people to the competitors. On the other hand, executive management can inspire confidence by anticipating problems and implementing corrective measures in an orderly way. Panic results from surprises, and the gravity of events during 1986–87 are clearly predictable. The competently managed B/Cs will be poised in 1988 to take full advantage of markets that are expanding worldwide.

9

Alternative Actions by Governments Worldwide

The avoidance of a financial crisis is primarily dependent on the American government's (1) recognizing that severe economic and financial problems could develop in 1986–87, (2) using its international influence to marshal forces to design a solution accepted by all creditor countries, and (3) implementing the steps necessary to save the banking system and maintain order in foreign exchange markets.

The probability of the three steps occurring in 1985 is very low. The Reagan administration is urging the Congress to retain a high level of defense spending and is refusing categorically to accept tax increases. Lobbying to save allocations for special interests has been feverish. The minor reduction in the FY1986 budget deficit will be overwhelmed by American government expenditures to implement the foreign debt solution, bolster the Federal Deposit Insurance Corporation, and contribute its share to international lending organizations that provide capital for global recovery. The irony of President Reagan's statement, "You ain't seen nothin' yet," will be apparent in 1986.

It will still be possible to prevent irrevocable damage to the global financial system by acting calmly and intelligently as the existence of a crisis becomes clear. However, the members of the Group of Ten other than the United States should make a concerted effort to influence President Reagan, his cabinet, and other officials to formulate contingency plans for the developments described in this book.

Even if the American government truly believes that no crisis is imminent, the fundamentals of management demand that such plans be prepared. If it is logical to have military contingency plans, why is it not logical to have detailed plans to circumvent a financial crisis? A foundering American economy is seriously damaging to the country's security.

The remainder of this chapter offers basic steps that governments can take to prepare for the crisis and minimize the impact on their economies. Two dimensions are covered. First, suggestions are made for a systematic evaluation of a nation's banking system. The second section deals with the fiscal and socioeconomic factors that must be considered as the crisis unfolds.

DAMAGE CONTROL IN THE BANKING SYSTEM

The technocrats in a country are fully aware of what must be done to prevent a bank panic. It is the politicians who are elected by the voters and who have ideological positions who will be obstacles in late 1985 and early 1986. At that stage, it will not be certain that there are global implications to an increased rate of bank failures in the United States and some bankruptcies in other countries. A consensus about actions to take will evolve in 1986, but a direct relationship exists between promptness and reduction of damaging affects.

The steps required include the following:

1. Bank examiners must determine the exact jeopardy of each lending institution in the country, private and public. The fact gathering includes foreign loans, standard domestic credit, and guaranteed loans involving government agencies. Each loan contract must be classified according to such categories as (a) de facto default, (b) nonperforming, (c) substandard debt service performance, (d) currently prompt, and (e) continuously prompt. The criteria placing a loan in one of the five categories must be defined clearly. A system for assessing country risk must supplement the criteria to support classifications of foreign loans.

If this step is politicized, the process is undermined. An example is the United States' upgrading the status of Argentine loans to "other transfer risk" from "substandard" after the 28 December 1984 rescheduling agreement. Chapter 3 clarified that it is impossible for the country to make prompt interest payments in the first year of the agree-

agreement. The new classification facilitated making fresh money available. However, it is blatantly absurd to assign such a rating.

2. A plan must be developed for each bank. It might be possible to have a standard plan for banks in condition X, another for condition Y, and so on, but all will require some tailoring to be certain that goals are realized. Mergers and acquisition of selected assets and liabilities by strong banks are likely to be required. Direct government involvement through guarantees, concessionary credits, and takeovers to save depositors could be involved in such extreme cases as the Continental Illinois rescue by the Federal Deposit Insurance Corporation.

The sum of the plans defines the scope of the government's commitment to securing the country's financial system. One aspect is the assignment of technocrats to assist bank executives in carrying out the plan; this could include a concentration of activities in certain types of businesses and elimination of others. Another aspect is the role of an intermediary in mergers and acquisitions to accelerate the process of reaching agreement. A third aspect is changes in the regulatory framework for banking activities.

3. Direct involvement with guarantees, special loans, and takeovers will usually require legislation. If only an isolated bank or two needs such assistance, the authority and budget of an existing agency might be sufficient to provide the necessary help in 1985–86. In most cases, the longer a government waits to implement the bank plans, the more costly it will be.

4. A public relations campaign will be necessary to build consensus for the restructuring of the banking system. Careful attention must be paid to communicating the benefits, minimizing the tendency to pinpoint blame, and creating a sense of security. Politicians who would exploit the situation for gains at the ballot box should be drawn into the early planning stages to make the program a multiparty effort. Accusations of the opposition should be anticipated and countertactics readied for possible use.

5. Uncovering irregularities, frauds, and conflicts of interest has a high probability of occurring. These should be handled by the appropriate law enforcement authorities, and consideration of the manner in which the wrongdoing is revealed should be part of the public relations campaign. Bad judgment must be separated from unethical and illegal acts to avoid including incompetent bank managers with people who must face charges. The media's tendency to seek a person to blame for each problem is likely to be counterproductive in implementing a comprehensive solution.

The decision to take Step 1 has major implications. Most politicians will be looking for an excuse to take the initiative. These could include (1) the failure or the rescuing of a major New York bank, (2) a sharp sustained fall in U.S. dollar exchange rates, (3) a major rise in the American prime rate (the next surge is predicted for the summer of 1985 to close the fiscal year), (4) a large drop in crude oil prices that affects debtor nations dependent on this commodity for debt service, and (5) a repeat of events in September 1982 (Mexico declared it could not pay its obligations), but involving more than one major debtor.

During the last half of 1986, all five motivations are likely to be taking place. It will be late for many creditor countries. Among the Group of Ten Germany and Switzerland have only a small task because of bad debt reserves already created, and these countries could wait until the crisis is obvious. Even with this timing, emergency actions required would be minimal. Japan has many more problems with foreign debts than these two countries, but the three have a low probability of a flood of domestic loans failing. France has taken preliminary steps as a result of the bank nationalizations, overborrowing in 1982–83, and austerity measures implemented in 1983 to correct imbalances. The United Kingdom has some jeopardy both from foreign and domestic loans, but technocratic competence is high, and the Conservative majority in parliament will permit appropriate action.

The problem country is the United States. The management of the country's fiscal and financial balances must be called irrational. The dedication to spending for defense and the refusal to legislate appropriate tax measures at a time of extraordinary deficits (budget and current account) borders on criminally irresponsible stewardship of the world's currency for international transactions. A strong defense is possible at lower levels of expenditures, and compromises on this issue would have achieved compromises by the opposition on social spending programs. Retrospectively, the Reagan years will be viewed as a financial disaster, despite the role that deficit spending played in the 1983–85 economic recovery.

FISCAL AND SOCIOECONOMIC STEPS

It is prudent for countries around the world to assume that the United States will not act until the scope of the crisis is clear and a consensus for countermeasures develops across party lines. This should be late 1986, about election time for the American Congress. The new representatives and senators will, therefore, be meeting in early 1987 to enact corrective legislation. By then the situation will be serious, and mistakes could result in a depression.

What do other governments do? During 1985–86 it is time to take strong defensive steps. These are discussed below.

Fiscal Measures

A major decline in revenues can be expected starting in mid-1986. Income taxes from individuals and companies, duties, and sources of earnings will be falling. Yet governments recognize from experience that it is difficult to trim spending in a recession for several reasons:

1. Budgets for recipients of public funds are fixed in advance, assuming no major change in amounts. These recipients range from the defense ministry to infrastructure maintenance at the local government level.
2. Members of parliament recognize that their political future depends on securing what has flowed into their constituency and adding to those amounts whenever possible.
3. Unemployment rises in a recession. Jobless rates have been high during the 1983–85 recovery period, but the numbers will grow significantly in 1986–87. Therefore, in addition to the chronically unemployed, a new strata of people will be added. Some will never have a real job again. Unemployment payments, training programs, and family relocation to new jobs will add to expenditures.
4. Make-work schemes will be necessary. Individuals need to be occupied for psychological reasons, as well as for purposes of income. Crime, violence, drug addictions, and other social problems escalate with idleness. Instead of allocating amounts for welfare payments, many countries will insist that recipients work for their money.
5. The year 1987 will be the worst year since the 1930s. Social conditions will be worse because of increased population density and large urban ghettos. Frustration and hopelessness will lead to violence. The need for security, law enforcement, and other city services will increase, and it is doubtful that local governments will have the revenue to provide what is required.
6. Every country will have growing debt service and projects under way that will need to be finished. This problem and special situations will add to the complications

of lowering budget deficits (few countries have surpluses).

It is apparent that governments will have severe fiscal troubles with decreasing revenues and increasing spending pressures. If nothing is done until 1987, the impact will be devastating. Some suggestions are given below, but no complete solution is known. Countries will be seeking degrees of controlling extremes and counteracting inflationary effects of higher deficits. These include:

- Plan budgets using such techniques as zero sum budgeting to establish priorities for every line item.
- Prepare a "bare bones" budget (bbb) that barely keeps the country functioning and maintains military security.
- Use the bbb as the basis for constructing the working budget, adding according to necessities as the situation evolves.
- Recognize the political realities; factor the positions of government party members, the opposition, media, and lobbying groups into the plans for implementation.
- Plan phased expenditure cuts. Reduce budget allocations in annual steps beginning in 1986.
- Review the current account debits for control opportunities; initiate measures that discourage (or prohibit) imports that are not essential (they should cover all invisibles, including unrequited transfers).
- Enact foreign exchange controls as required; take steps necessary to intervene on convertible currency transactions deemed detrimental to the state's interests.
- Institute an employment freeze. Reduce government employment through attrition.
- Freeze wages, or establish a mechanism for subinflationary increases.
- Reschedule debt service obligations to reduce principal payments in the 1986–88 period.
- Refinance loans to obtain lower interest rates and adequate grace periods to avoid debt service becoming a larger percentage of the total.

A global gap exists between the budgets prepared by technocrats with objectivity and those desired by politicians with vested interests. It is often the case that members of the executive and parliamentary divisions of government have little formal training in economics. Some even mistrust the technocrats who have prepared wrong forecasts as a basis for policy. Therefore, the people competent to prepare an emergency budget systematically will encounter considerable political and military resistance until a broad consensus develops.

To initiate steps well in advance of the crisis, the support of a strong leader is necessary. This is possible in such countries as Korea, Singapore, and Taiwan. Democracies in which the prime minister has a strong majority are also possibilities for taking firm action; these include Spain, Turkey, and the United Kingdom. Fragmented political structures or those under pressure for change are less likely to take early steps.

Tactical Measures

The suggestions given below assume that the governments in power will be (1) highly criticized, (2) the objects of strikes, demonstrations, and riots, and (3) attacked by guerrilla groups, terrorists, and cells devoted to various causes. In Japan, Norway, and Switzerland, the incidents will be mild and infrequent. France and Germany will have terrorist bombings, kidnappings, and strikes. Current problems in other countries will be aggravated. Summarizing, socioeconomic conditions will be extremely bad for about a year, and governments have the responsibility to maintain order for the majority of citizens who do not participate in disruptive actions. Steps include:

- Strengthen the internal intelligence apparatus; stress professionals, but use local party cadre as a source of early warning information.
- Prepare for crowd control and terrorist actions as thoroughly as Los Angeles did for the 1984 Olympic Games:
  - Consider psychopathic responses to personal problems.
  - Develop policies and responses to massive or violent job actions and lockouts.
  - Train police and paramilitary forces for responses to riots involving planned resistance, multiple injuries, and property damage.
  - Establish policies for ransom demands, treatment of forces holding hostages, and other forms of intimidation by organized gangs.
  - Create special police units for assaults, rescues, and protection of key personnel.
  - Encourage the media to develop a self-restraint code that all agree to observe during emergencies.
- Instruct the central bank to plan for the foreign debt solution by having prepared the organizational structure, the sequence of steps to take under alternative

solutions, and the officials to be responsible for the plan.

- Consider the probability and reaction to a neighboring nation initiating military action against the country to defuse political turmoil at home.
- Plan humanitarian measures including food stations, shelter for the homeless, centers for abandoned children, and other allowances for extremely poor social conditions; in cases where the numbers of desperate people exceed the budget, establish procedures for those qualifying for assistance.
- Enlarge safety stocks for energy, essential processing, and nutrition as resources permit to allow for infrastructure breakdowns, terrorist acts, and other interruptions of normal supplies.

These suggestions allow for (1) low probability acts, (2) a small number of people having the capacity to disrupt a country, (3) retaliation against society by individuals hurt by the crisis, (4) multiple strikes similar in scope to the 1984–85 British coal miners walkout, and (5) some exaggeration of current subversive activities by assassination squads, guerrilla operations, and organized crime, including drug trafficking, and terrorism. It does not take a major increase in the level of the five categories to create chaos.

Psychological Measures

People can become very apprehensive about important future events and lose sight of reality. Deception and manipulation rarely can be justified, but the population can be competently prepared for deep recession. Furthermore, the process can generate support for fiscal and tactical measures. Most important, when the solution to the worldwide financial crisis is submitted to the public in a referendum or to parliament (congress, house, or appropriate title), greater understanding about the gravity of the matter will assist in obtaining approval.

The checklist suggested below will have to be supplemented by items that relate to individual countries. It will be essential to have the support of the media during the emergency. Most people will not understand why their living standards have declined sharply and why many people are suffering extreme hardship. Some of the ideas to be considered are:

- Involve the media methodically; however, confine journalist interviews with technocrats to topics about the research, techniques employed, alternative scenarios, and interpretations of what is happening in other countries. Leave the results, alternative actions, and specific proposals to leaders who are accustomed to dealing with reporters. The goal is to gain credibility, confidence about the approach to problem solving, and favorable attitudes toward those government officials involved in conceiving and implementing the measures. Realistically, avoiding frequent attacks by journalists and limiting the degree of alienation by the voters is likely to be the best that can be expected.

- Influence public opinion on key points and sensitive areas. Consistency of policy, posture, and statements is critical. Carefully select the information to be released, the timing (including frequency), and the people involved in handling the campaign. One of these points should be the theme "It is unsatisfactory here, but remember what is happening in Country X and Country Y." Attitudes can be improved by emphasizing that local conditions are superior to that in nations with comparable industries, standards, and so on.
- Secure the support of important power factors. This involves credible information selected for the target group. The techniques involve confidential memos, briefings on developments, social occasions to leak probable future events, and such other tactics as working breakfasts and one-on-one meetings. The psychological approach could include intimidation in the process of releasing information. Those involved with securing support must balance the favorable with the unfavorable to avoid loss of creditability.
- Use the public positions of ethnic/language, racial/religious groups to further the government's position whenever possible. Mix the securing of support from the leaders of these groups and the students, unions, military, police, and others with efforts to reach the body of the groups with the selected message. The key element is that progress with the leaders is reinforced by support from their membership.

Challenge from the Author

Assigning blame is a luxury that the world cannot afford. The period of 1985–86 is a time for action. It is necessary for members of the Group of Ten to prepare a detailed solution for the foreign debt problem. If the Reagan administration wishes to concentrate American creative energy on military and diplomatic affairs, then the other ten members should take steps to design a response to events that are only months away.

The professionals at the Bank of International Settlements could start the process. The IMF is deeply involved in the adjustment programs for debtor nations. Consequently, it would be appropriate for the Group of Ten to:

1. Commission the BIS to prepare the framework for a solution and present it to the Group of Ten at the first 1986 meeting.
2. Form a liaison committee of Group of Ten technocrats and instruct this committee to work with the BIS to refine the framework and to resolve preliminary objections. (Include an American on this committee regardless of the government's position on the need for a solution).
3. Present a revised framework for the solution at a spring 1986 Group of Ten meeting. Provide alternatives if the committee divides on certain issues. Resolve the differences on approach.
4. Authorize the BIS and the liaison committee to complete a detailed solution for presentation at a fall 1986 Group of Ten meeting.
5. Have an approved foreign debt solution in the form of a complete contingency plan ready by end-1986.

It is probable that this schedule will have to be accelerated. The condition of many banks in the United States will be worrisome by mid-1986. This is likely to prod the Reagan administration into taking a more active role in the liaison committee. Using network modeling to control the timing of several individual contributors, the solution could be ready by fall 1986.

A tenacious leader in combination with a respected technocrat must insist on the contingency plan being prepared. If the process can be begun in late 1985 or early 1986, considerable suffering can be avoided. The author urges one of the Group of Ten leaders to accept this challenge.

Appendixes

Appendix A: Assessment of Human Resources

METHODOLOGY

Sixty members of the Operations Risk Index and Political Risk Index panels of BERI S.A. were randomly selected and requested to reply for the countries that they rate for the measures. All replies were received in 1984. A minimum of five replies per country proved to be statistically significant. Each of the nine variables were rated from 0 (worst case) to 10 (best case). Ten weighting points could be applied at the discretion of the panel member. A perfect score is too.

Scale

0 — 100

0	100	P	0-4	5-9	P	0-4	5-9	P	0-4	5-9	P	0-4	5-9	P	0-4	5-9
1. Emotional Tendency toward Violence	Disciplined/Pragmatic Capacity to Compromise	___	___	___	___	___	___	___	___	___	___	___	___	___	___	___
2. Pervasive Corruption	Minimal Corruption	___	___	___	___	___	___	___	___	___	___	___	___	___	___	___
3. Untrained Work Force/Low Educational Level	Skilled Workers High Educational Level	___	___	___	___	___	___	___	___	___	___	___	___	___	___	___
4. Low Interest in Work Narrow Span of Control Business Held in Low Esteem	Strong Work Ethic Problem-solving Capability Entrepreneurism	___	___	___	___	___	___	___	___	___	___	___	___	___	___	___
5. Highly Structured Culture Options Linked to Tradition	Flexible Independent Personal Behavior Class Distinctions Based on Individual Performance	___	___	___	___	___	___	___	___	___	___	___	___	___	___	___

P = Present, 0-4 and 5-9 Years in the Future

6. Classism/Elitism Poor Wealth Distribution	Broad Wealth Distribution	___ ___ ___ ___ ___ ___ ___ ___ ___ ___ ___ ___ ___ ___ ___
7. High Fractionalization by Language, Ethnic Group, or Religion	Low Fractionalization by Language, Ethnic Group, or Religion	___ ___ ___ ___ ___ ___ ___ ___ ___ ___ ___ ___ ___ ___ ___
8. State Owned Enterprise Xenophobia	Private Free Enterprise Minimal Restrictions on Foreign Investment	___ ___ ___ ___ ___ ___ ___ ___ ___ ___ ___ ___ ___ ___ ___
9. High Fractionalization by by Ideology or Region	Low Fractionalization by Ideology or Region	___ ___ ___ ___ ___ ___ ___ ___ ___ ___ ___ ___ ___ ___ ___
Weighting Option*	________________	
Weighting Option*	________________	
	TOTALS	

*Any of the nine human variables may be selected to give additional weighting. Discretionary points may be awarded in any variable, but only a total of ten points may be allocated for weighting

Appendix B: User Guide of BERI S.A.'s FORELEND Service

FORELEND is a service which provides qualitative analyses and quantitative ratings for decision making about:

(1) Terms and structure of new loans.
(2) Participation in syndications.
(3) Rescheduling terms and negotiating objectives.
(4) Extending credit on purchases of goods and services.
(5) Financial factors such as committing to guarantees and the timing of progress payments in construction contracts.

The emphasis is on a +5 years forecast for each of the 50 countries. Ratings and reasons for predicted conditions are given. The present situation and five years of historical data are provided for independent trend analysis.

FORELEND uses a sensitive measure of a country's capacity and willingness to meet its contractual obligations in convertible currency. This measure is called LR, an acronym for Lender's Risk Rating. LR has the 1 (prime borrower) to 8 (de factor default) range that is shown on the next page. The eight ratings are based on a composite score for a country, and components and methods for compiling this score are explained in the next section of the User Guide. Each LR has a "Recommended User Action." Countries with LR1 to LR4 receive "lend" recommendations; but risk increases as LR increases, and recommended terms reflect higher levels of risk. Countries with LR5 or more should receive neither new loans nor credit on purchases. In the case of a LR5 country, jeopardy to principal is generally to great regardless of the premium obtained on interest rates, profit margins, etc., but a valid foreign party guarantee may justify credit and loans in individual cases.

The "Saturation Factor is a theoretical calculation and is not part of LR. It is a supplementary measure which is cited frequently in qualitative analyses of net oil importing countries. A country reaches saturation when debt service plus imports of petroleum are 80% or more of foreign exchange earned. No new convertible currency funds should be loaned to a country in this situation. An explanation of the "Saturation Factor" is given in the last section of the User Guide.

Composite Score	LR	Recommended Lender Action	Country Performance on Loans
65-100	1	Lend. Prime borrower.	Prompt principal and interest payments.
60-64	2	Lend at rate higher than the rate offered to a prime borrower.	Future obligations will be paid on schedule.
56-59	3	Lend at high rate. Generally tighten terms. Require government guarantee on loans to private parties.	
50-54	4	Lend at highest rate. Require foreign bank or foreign government guarantee.	Principal and interest payments presently on schedule. Promptness in future jeopardized by predicted conditions.
45-49	5	Offer no new funds. Avoid rollovers. Consistently seek recovery of principal.	
40-44	6	Implement expediting tactics on interest payments. Prepare rescheduling strategy.	Interest payments on schedule. Principal payments sometimes delayed.
35-39	7	Prepare "worst case" actions. Control time and expenses allocated to recovery of funds.	Interest payments sometimes delayed. Principal payments require rescheduling.
0-34	8	Selectively implement "worst case" actions. Control time and expenses allocated to recovery of funds.	De facto default. Interest payments capitalized. Restructuring.

DETERIORATING COUNTRY PERFORMANCE ON LOANS

COMPOSITION OF THE COMPOSITE SCORE

The composite score, which is the basis of a country's LR, establishes a quantitative framework for the two-page qualitative analysis of each country. It involves three components which measure the causes of lender risk in a country.

1. A wholly quantitative rating integrates statistics on

performance in generating foreign exchange, maintaining reserve levels, accumulating foreign debt, balancing budgets, and other related factors. Reliable, regularly published data by the International Monetary Fund, World Bank, and similar sources are used. This measure is called LRquant.

2. A wholly qualitative rating has been created to evaluate technocratic competence, loan structure, related regulatory framework, sensitive issues such as corruption and resolve to honor international obligations. The regular monitory of the 50 countries by the BERI S.A. research team provides criteria ratings. A structured format is used, and the Delphi method acts as a quality control mechanism. This measure is called LRqual.

3. A rating which moves independently of LRquant and LRqual has been created from BERI S.A.'s panel-based political and operations risk indexes to assess the political and socio-economic situation in each country. Criteria have been selected to tailor the assessment to the international lender's perspective. Social indicators, such as per capita daily calorie consumption, are 20% of the rating. This measure is called LRenvir.

LRquant is 50% of LR. LRqual and LRenvir make up the other half, each contributing 25%. This composition gives equal emphasis to criteria for which statistics are available and for those which require subjective judgment. An example of a composite score is given below using Korea's (ROK) ratings for 1982:

LRquant	46 x 50% =	23.00
LRqual	57 x 25% =	14.25
LRenvir	54 x 25% =	13.50
Composite Score		51 (rounded)
LR		4

Note that all ratings are rounded to the nearest whole number. Countries on the threshold of another LR rating will be monitored continuously, especially when the change is from LR4 to LR5, and these will be the bases of Client Alerts throughout the year.

All three measures--LRquant, LRqual, and LRenvir--use the same risk scale. This is shown schematically below:

Prohibitive	High	Moderate	Low
0 — 35	35 — 50	50 — 85	85 — 100

LRquant (50% of LR)

The purpose of LRquant is to estimate a country's capacity to meet its contractual obligations in convertible currency. This includes both public and private obligations. The computer program manipulates over 15,000 cells of data and makes hundreds of calculations for each LRquant rating and the four subindexes described below.

1. Foreign Exchange Generation Subindex (30% of LRquant). IMF data published in "International Financial Statistics" (IMF) are used. Certain statistics were converted to standard normal variates. This technique makes meaningful comparisons possible despite an immense range in the data across the countries.

- Current account performance is the critical component of the subindex, receiving 80 points. Breakeven receives 40 points. A two-year rolling average is used to dampen the impact of unusual years.
- Capital flows receive up to a maximum of 20 points by establishing breakeven as 10.

2. Foreign Debt Assessment Subindex (30% of LRquant). The World Bank's "World Debt Tables" are the starting point for developing data on public foreign debt of developing countries. Industrialized countries also require several sources, primarily central bank reports.

- A ratio using gross domestic product converted to US$ as the denominator is used to put the debt into perspective with the economy. Creditor nations receive all 50 points; the largest result receives zero.
- Capacity to service debt is measured by a ration of annual public foreign loan obligations (numerator) and foreign exchange earned as the denominator. Fifty points go to creditor nations.

3. Accumulated International Reserves Subindex (30% of LRquant).

- First, months of coverage for imports of merchandise and services are used as a means of relating hard currency reserves to scope of needs. The most coverage each year receives 50 points; the smallest fraction of a month earns zero.

- Second, the international reserve total is added to the London valuation for gold holdings to give a complete total on reserves. A ratio is then calculated using total public foreign debt as the numerator.

4. Budget Performance Subindex (10% of LRquant). "Government Finance Statistics Yearbook" data published by IMF are used. The annual data are updated in the IFS in most instances.

- Deficit/surplus of the national budget as a decimal of gross domestic product. Surplus or breakdown receives 30 points; 0.09 (9%) or more receives zero.
- Percent growth of revenues minus percent growth of expenditures. Three-year rolling averages. Zero (percentages are equal) receives 20 points. Positive results receive up to 40 points in increments of 0.5%; negative results decrease incrementally to zero.
- Expenditures as a decimal of gross domestic product. 0.10 or less receives all 30 points; one point is lost for each 0.01 over 0.10. Therefore, 0.40 or more receives zero.

Data used for the +5 years forecast are the result of regression analysis, research staff input based on scenarios in the FORCE reports, trends in the ratings, and senior staff judgment. Forecasts using wholly quantitative techniques proved unrealistic.

LRqual (25% of LR)

The objective of the index is to measure factors which have a direct influence on meeting international obligations but which cannot be assessed through regularly published statistics. The net impact of different value systems, religious practices, traditions, etc., from the viewpoint of the international lender is also estimated by LRqual. The criteria used in LRqual are identified below:

	Weighting
Level of resolve toward honoring international obligations	3
Foreign loan structure and terms:	
Range, concessionary to short term	2
Current market terms	1
Net technological competence:	
Overall assessment	2½
Political interference	1½

Corruption in financial transactions:	
Direct fraud	2
Indirect diversion of funds	1½
Concessionary loans and grants:	
Level of access	1½
Influence of strategic importance	1½
Legal framework:	
Convertibility for principal, interest and fees	2
Taxation constraints	1½
	20

The 11 criteria have a weighted total of 20. Each criterion for each country is rated from 5 (best case) to zero (worst case). Therefore, a perfect country would receive 100 (20 x 5). The research and analysis undertaken to develop historical data beginning in 1978 required many man-years of effort. Countries most typical of a zero, 1, 2, etc., rating for each criterion in each year were selected and used as a basis of comparison to rate the other countries. The accumulated expertise and information are being applied to other current LRqual ratings and the forecasts. A version of the Delphi technique is being used to obtain convergence with staff ratings.

The forecasts do not involve criterion-by-criterion ratings. Instead, the staff estimates LRqual in +5 years using a single number, such as 57. A mean of the contributions is used after the senior staff estimates are given double weighting. Experience with forecasting other ratings indicates that this method results in the most meaningful predictions.

LRenvir (25% of LR)

This measure has three components: (1) BERI S.A.'s Political Risk Index, 40%; (2) selected criteria with adjust weightings from the Operations Risk Index, 40%; and (3) a Social Conditions Subindex with eight commonly used criteria for gauging the quality of living conditions, 20%. The purpose of LRenvir is to evaluate the political and socioeconomic environment. The production of goods and services needed to pay foreign creditors depends upon this environment. The content and methodology involved in each of the three components are explained below:

1. Political Risk Index (40% of LRenvir). The index focuses wholly on sociopolitical conditions in a country. It uses a multicomponent system with flexibility to weight key factors. A permanent panel of 75 political scientists and diplomats provide data which can move independently of other risk measures. Two time periods are involved: present conditions and conditions in five years.

First Step in the System. The expert rates the present conditions for each of the eight causes show below from 7 (no problems) to zero (prohibitive problems). Then, the two symptoms are rated on the same scale in the present. The perspective is from the viewpoint of an international bank rather than private enterprise owned by nationals. This subtotal involves a maximum of 70 for the perfect country.

Six Internal Causes of Political Risk:
- Fractionalization of the political spectrum and the power of these factions.
- Fractionalization by language, ethnic and/or religious groups and the power of these factions.
- Restrictive (coercive) measures required to retain power.
- Mentality, including xenophobia, nationalism, corruption, nepotism, willingness to compromise.
- Social conditions, including population density and wealth distribution.
- Organization and strength of forces for a radical left government.

Two External Causes of Political Risk:
- Dependence on and/or importance to a hostile major power.
- Negative influences of regional political forces.

Two Symptoms of Political Risk:
- Societal conflict involving demonstrations, strikes, and street violence.
- Instability as perceived by nonconstitutional changes, assassinations, and guerrilla wars.

Second Step in the System. One or more of the causes may have an overwhelming impact on the overall political risk. The second subtotal of the system allocates a total of 30 risk points to causes (not symptoms). The expert can apply the risk points to one, two, etc., causes or opt to allocate no additional risk points. The completely risky country would receive a rating of 100 as a result of Steps One and Two.

Forecast of RPI. Steps One and Two are repeated for the +5 years period. The points given to a country under present conditions serve as a basis for changes in the future.

2. Adjusted Operations Risk Index (40% of LRenvir). The objective of this index is to gauge the business operations climate. There are two variables being measured: (1) the degree to which nations are given preferential treatment and (2) the general quality of the business climate. A permanent panel of ±105 experts around the world rate present conditions for the 15 criteria which make up a cross-section of the country's business climate. Eight of the 15 have been selected because of relevance to lender risk. These criteria are shown below. Each is rated from zero

(unacceptable conditions) to 4 (superior conditions). The criteria are weighted to emphasize important factors, and this expands the eight to a weighted total of 25. A rating of 4 on each criterion gives a perfect environment of 100.

The quality of the panel is the foundation of the concept. Executives in companies, banks, governments, and institutions volunteer their ratings. All have extensive international experience. Geographic distribution is worldwide. A version of the Delphi method is used. Data are from a permanent panel. The first reply prepared by a panel member requires research and care in matching the rating with the definitions of the criteria. A panelist is supplied with his previous reply and the overall panel average per criterion as input for decisions on current ratings.

Each panel member rates a country for a +5 years period by giving a whole number for the overall rating, such as 70, 62, etc. The high and the low ORI forecasts are discarded, and a panelwide average is used.

	Weighting
Monetary inflation	4
Bureaucratic delays	3½
Economic growth	5
Enforceability of contracts	3½
Professional services and contractors	1
Communications and transportation	3
Short-term credit	2½
Long-term loans and venture capital	2½
	25

3. Social Condition Subindex (20% of LRenvir). The eight criteria shown below are measured quantitatively. The mean for the 50 countries receives a rating of 5 in each criterion. An increment is established for data above and below the mean, thereby establishing a basis for increasing the rating to a maximum of 10 and decreasing it to zero. The eight criteria have a weighted total of 10, and a perfect country has a rating of 100 (10 x 10).

	Weighting
Per capita income in US$s	2
Government spending for social development per capital	1
Unemployment rate	1
Adult literacy rate	1
Population growth	2
Per capita daily calorie consumption	1
Life expectancy	1
Infant mortality	1
	10

The five-year forecast is a BERI S.A. staff estimate. The historical data indicate that the subindex fluctuates within a narrow amplitude. Therefore, the forecasts have a high probability of being accurate.

SATURATION FACTOR

The "Saturation Factor" is a theoretical calculation in US$s. It uses the cost of net oil imports and debt service on foreign loans as the numerator and foreign exchange generated from merchandise and service exports plus net unrequited transfers as the denominator. A country is fully saturated when the result is 80% or more. The following three categories describe conditions at various degrees of saturation.

1. Over 60% of foreign exchange generation is going to oil purchases and debt service. Severe austerity measures are required, and rescheduling of principal payments is necessary. Future growth is limited by inadequate capital to expand or even maintain the present economic infrastructure. The sociopolitical framework is potentially unstable as a result of steps to meet obligations. Current examples using 1981 data include Brazil, 104%; Turkey, 67%; and Zaire, 69%.

2. Between 31% and 60% of foreign exchange is going to oil purchases and debt service. Expansion of the economy and real GDP growth over 3% causes untenable energy consumption, current account deficits, increased foreign debt, and accelerated inflation. Policies to avoid these problems fend to cause unemployment, high interest rates, and low levels of investment. Countries with more than 1% net population growth rates and unstable political systems will tend to take steps which increase their saturation measure; in these cases, social unrest also increases and management of the economy becomes difficult. Those with a tendency to increase, for example, include (1891 data) Korea (ROK), 42%; Philippines, 44%; and Portugal, 33%.

3. Up to 30% of foreign exchange is going to oil purchases and debt service. Competitiveness of advanced countries has been generally hurt by the 1160% oil increase during 1974-81, but some countries have done a remarkable job of management. For example, the 1981 Saturation Measure for Taiwan (ROC) was 15%. On the other hand, Sweden was moving towards the 31% to 60% category with 26%.

The "Saturation Factor" does not apply to net oil exporting countries. A substitute measure involving net food imports instead of oil is being developed.

Copyright © 1985 BERI S.A.
No portion of this report is to be reproduced in any form without written permission from the publisher.

Index

About the Author

F. T. Haner, 55, formed BERI S.A. in 1966 and is currently its president. Dr. Haner is also Distinguished Professor of Business and Economics at Whittier College, California. In parallel activities during the past two decades, he was a professor at the University of Delaware (1971–80), co-founded and managed an agribusiness in Portugal (1968–71), and assisted Litton Industries' economic development effort as Managing Director of Litton Benelux S.A. (1967–68).

Previously, he started American Cement's international division and was responsible for profitable operations in Greece and Spain. Experience gained at Stanford Research Institute (1959–62) and U.S. Steel (1955–59) also played a role in BERI's success in conceiving and marketing information for international business. Dr. Haner has conducted feasibility studies, negotiated terms, and managed companies in 37 countries around the world.

He has authored seven books, the latest two being *Country Risk Assessment: Theory and Worldwide Practice* and *The Financial Crisis: Causes and a Proposed Solution*. Both will be published in 1985. In addition to the statistical measures of risk and forecasts of conditions in 62 countries published by Dr. Haner through BERI S.A., he has written several articles on international management and strategic planning.

He received his Ph.D. in econometrics at the University of Pittsburgh in 1959. His undergraduate degree was in petroleum geology from the University of Michigan. Dr. Haner enjoys ocean sailboat racing and plays racquetball for exercise.